ENGLISH TEXTS

Edited by
Theo Stemmler

3

Elizabethan Sonnet
Sequences

Edited
by
Herbert Grabes

MAX NIEMEYER VERLAG TÜBINGEN

1970

CONTENTS

Preface V

Sir Philip Sidney, *Astrophel and Stella* . . 1

Samuel Daniel, *Delia* 65

Michael Drayton, *Ideas Mirrovr* 89

Edmund Spenser, *Amoretti* 119

Textual Sources 158

Bibliography 159

ISBN 3 484 44002 3

© Max Niemeyer Verlag Tübingen 1970
Alle Rechte vorbehalten. Printed in Germany
Satz: Karl Schenk Reutlingen-Sondelfingen
Druck: Karl Grammlich Pliezhausen

PREFACE

When faced with the task of acquainting a group of students with the Elizabethan sonnet, one soon notices that a suitable, low-priced collection of texts is lacking. There is, of course, a great number of anthologies containing many sonnets from the Elizabethan period, but in offering only those sonnets which literary criticism or the editors deem better or more typical than the rest, they neglect the fact that it is not the single sonnet, but the sonnet cycle or sequence that is typical of Elizabethan sonnet-writing. It is true that any poem is a self-contained work of art, and this applies particularly to the sonnet; but this if anything renders more important the poets' attempt to build these independent units into larger wholes.

If this is obvious enough, what remains is the task of choosing from the many sequences that have come down to us. Judged by their literary merits, Shakespeare's *Sonnets* rank first, but apart from the fact that here we do not know whether we have a sonnet cycle or just 'collected sonnets' they are omitted because most students will possess the text in their *Works of Shakespeare* or can easily obtain it. The second choice would combine Spenser's *Amoretti* and Sidney's *Astrophel and Stella*, the latter not only for its intrinsic value, but also for its historical importance as an impetus to the fashion of sonnet-writing; followed by Daniel's *Delia* and Drayton's *Idea*. These cycles show the Elizabethan sonnet at its best and offer so much variety in the way of invention and style that they can be considered a fair choice from the cycles of the period and an adequate basis for an appreciation of them.

The texts of the first editions of these cycles, as used in the following collection with the exception of *Astrophel and Stella*, also represent the brief peak of Elizabethan sonnet-writing in the years 1591-95. For *Astrophel and Stella* W. A. Ringler's critical text based on the 1598 version in the Countess of Pembroke's *Arcadia* is used, because the two pirated editions of 1591 are incomplete; for Daniel's *Delia* and Spenser's *Amoretti* the texts of the first editions of 1592 and 1595 respectively are in any case preferable to the others. Although Drayton's cycle is usually offered in the frequently revised version of the *Collected Poems* of 1619 rather than that of the first edition of 1594 offered here, and although the final version is undoubtedly superior in literary value, that of the first edition is for all its 'Elizabethan exuberance' more typical than the final product of numerous alterations and revisions, which were at least partly dictated by later stylistic fashions.

H.G.

Astrophel and Stella

Written by

The Noble Knight

Sir Philip Sidney

1 LOVING in truth, and faine in verse my love to show,
That the deare She might take some pleasure of my paine:
Pleasure might cause her reade, reading might make her know,
Knowledge might pitie winne, and pitie grace obtaine,
    I sought fit words to paint the blackest face of woe,
Studying inventions fine, her wits to entertaine:
Oft turning others' leaves, to see if thence would flow
Some fresh and fruitfull showers upon my sunne-burn'd braine.
    But words came halting forth, wanting Invention's stay,
Invention, Nature's child, fled step-dame Studie's blowes,
And others' feete still seem'd but strangers in my way.
Thus great with child to speake, and helplesse in my throwes,
    Biting my trewand pen, beating my selfe for spite,
    'Foole,' said my Muse to me, 'looke in thy heart and write.'

2 NOT at first sight, nor with a dribbed shot
    Love gave the wound, which while I breathe will bleed:
    But knowne worth did in mine of time proceed,
Till by degrees it had full conquest got.
I saw and liked, I liked but loved not,
    I loved, but straight did not what *Love* decreed:
    At length to *Love's* decrees, I forc'd, agreed,
Yet with repining at so partiall lot.
    Now even that footstep of lost libertie
Is gone, and now like slave-borne *Muscovite,*
I call it praise to suffer Tyrannie;
And now employ the remnant of my wit,
    To make my selfe beleeve, that all is well,
    While with a feeling skill I paint my hell.

3

LET daintie wits crie on the Sisters nine,
That bravely maskt, their fancies may be told:
Or *Pindare's* Apes, flaunt they in phrases fine,
Enam'ling with pied flowers their thoughts of gold:
    Or else let them in statelier glorie shine,
Ennobling new found Tropes with problemes old:
Or with strange similies enrich each line,
Of herbes or beastes, which *Inde* or *Afrike* hold.
    For me in sooth, no Muse but one I know:
    Phrases and Problemes from my reach do grow,
And strange things cost too deare for my poore sprites.
    How then? even thus: in *Stella's* face I reed,
    What Love and Beautie be, then all my deed
But Copying is, what in her Nature writes.

4

VERTUE alas, now let me take some rest,
Thou setst a bate betweene my will and wit,
If vaine love have my simple soule opprest,
Leave what thou likest not, deale not thou with it.
    Thy scepter use in some old *Catoe's* brest;
Churches or schooles are for thy seate more fit:
I do confesse, pardon a fault confest,
My mouth too tender is for thy hard bit.
    But if that needs thou wilt usurping be,
    The litle reason that is left in me,
And still th'effect of thy perswasions prove:
    I sweare, my heart such one shall shew to thee,
    That shrines in flesh so true a Deitie,
That *Vertue,* thou thy selfe shalt be in love.

5

IT is most true, that eyes are form'd to serve
The inward light: and that the heavenly part
Ought to be king, from whose rules who do swerve,
Rebels to Nature, strive for their owne smart.
    It is most true, what we call *Cupid's* dart,
An image is, which for our selves we carve;
And, fooles, adore in temple of our hart,
Till that good God make Church and Churchman starve.

4

True, that true Beautie Vertue is indeed,
Whereof this Beautie can be but a shade,
Which elements with mortall mixture breed:
True, that on earth we are but pilgrims made,
    And should in soule up to our countrey move:
    True, and yet true that I must *Stella* love.

6 SOME Lovers speake when they their Muses entertaine,
Of-hopes begot by feare, of wot not what desires:
Of force of heav'nly beames, infusing hellish paine:
Of living deaths, deare wounds, faire stormes and freesing fires:
    Some one his song in *Jove*, and *Jove's* strange tales attires,
Broadred with buls and swans, powdred with golden raine:
Another humbler wit to shepheard's pipe retires,
Yet hiding royall bloud full oft in rurall vaine.
    To some a sweetest plaint, a sweetest stile affords,
    While teares powre out his inke, and sighs breathe out his words:
His paper, pale dispaire, and paine his pen doth move.
    I can speake what I feele, and feele as much as they,
    But thinke that all the Map of my state I display,
When trembling voice brings forth that I do *Stella* love.

7 WHEN Nature made her chiefe worke, *Stella's* eyes,
In colour blacke, why wrapt she beames so bright?
Would she in beamie blacke, like painter wise,
Frame daintiest lustre, mixt of shades and light?
    Or did she else that sober hue devise,
In object best to knit and strength our sight,
Least if no vaile those brave gleames did disguise,
They sun-like should more dazle then delight?
    Or would she her miraculous power show,
That whereas blacke seemes Beautie's contrary,
She even in blacke doth make all beauties flow?
Both so and thus, she minding *Love* should be
    Placed ever there, gave him this mourning weed,
    To honor all their deaths, who for her bleed.

8   *LOVE* borne in *Greece,* of late fled from his native place,
      Forc'd by a tedious proofe, that Turkish hardned hart,
      Is no fit marke to pierce with his fine pointed dart:
    And pleasd with our soft peace, staid here his flying race.
    But finding these North clymes do coldly him embrace,
      Not usde to frozen clips, he strave to find some part,
      Where with most ease and warmth he might employ his art:
    At length he perch'd himself in *Stella's* joyfull face,
      Whose faire skin, beamy eyes, like morning sun on snow,
    Deceiv'd the quaking boy, who thought from so pure light,
    Effects of lively heat, must needs in nature grow.
    But she most faire, most cold, made him thence take his flight
      To my close heart, where while some firebrands he did lay,
      He burnt unwares his wings, and cannot fly away.

9   QUEENE *Vertue's* court, which some call *Stella's* face,
      Prepar'd by Nature's chiefest furniture,
      Hath his front built of Alablaster pure;
    Gold is the covering of that stately place.
    The doore by which sometimes comes forth her Grace,
      Red Porphir is, which locke of pearle makes sure:
      Whose porches rich (which name of cheekes endure)
    Marble mixt red and white do enterlace.
    The windowes now through which this heav'nly guest
    Looks over the world, and can find nothing such,
    Which dare claime from those lights the name of best,
    Of touch they are that without touch doth touch,
      Which *Cupid's* selfe from Beautie's myne did draw:
      Of touch they are, and poore I am their straw.

10   REASON, in faith thou art well serv'd, that still
    Wouldst brabling be with sence and love in me:
    I rather wisht thee clime the Muses' hill,
    Or reach the fruite of Nature's choisest tree,
      Or seeke heavn's course, or heavn's inside to see:
    Why shouldst thou toyle our thornie soile to till?
    Leave sense, and those which sense's objects be:
    Deale thou with powers of thoughts, leave love to will.

But thou wouldst needs fight both with love and sence,
With sword of wit, giving wounds of dispraise,
Till downe-right blowes did foyle thy cunning fence:
For soone as they strake thee with *Stella's* rayes,
　　Reason thou kneel'dst, and offeredst straight to prove
　　By reason good, good reason her to love.

1　IN truth, ô Love, with what a boyish kind
　　　Thou doest proceed in thy most serious wayes:
　　　That when the heav'n to thee his best displayes,
　　Yet of that best thou leav'st the best behind.
　　For like a child that some faire booke doth find,
　　　With guilded leaves or colourd Velume playes,
　　　Or at the most on some fine picture stayes,
　　But never heeds the fruit of writer's mind:
　　　So when thou saw'st in Nature's cabinet
　　Stella, thou straight lookst babies in her eyes,
　　In her cheeke's pit thou didst thy pitfould set,
　　And in her breast bopeepe or couching lyes,
　　　Playing and shining in each outward part:
　　　But, foole, seekst not to get into her hart.

2　*CUPID,* because thou shin'st in *Stella's* eyes,
　　　That from her lockes, thy day-nets, none scapes free,
　　　That those lips swell, so full of thee they bee,
　　That her sweete breath makes oft thy flames to rise,
　　That in her breast thy pap well sugred lies,
　　　That her Grace gracious makes thy wrongs, that she
　　　What words so ere she speakes perswades for thee,
　　That her cleare voyce lifts thy fame to the skies.
　　　Thou countest *Stella* thine, like those whose powers
　　Having got up a breach by fighting well,
　　Crie, 'Victorie, this faire day all is ours.'
　　O no, her heart is such a Cittadell,
　　　So fortified with wit, stor'd with disdaine,
　　　That to win it, is all the skill and paine.

13 *PHOEBUS* was Judge betweene *Jove, Mars,* and *Love,*
　　Of those three gods, whose armes the fairest were:
　　Jove's golden shield did Eagle sables beare,
Whose talents held young *Ganimed* above:
But in Vert field *Mars* bare a golden speare,
　　Which through a bleeding heart his point did shove:
　　Each had his creast, *Mars* caried *Venus'* glove,
Jove on his helme the thunderbolt did reare.
　　Cupid then smiles, for on his crest there lies
　　　Stella's faire haire, her face he makes his shield,
　　　Where roses gueuls are borne in silver field.
Phœbus drew wide the curtaines of the skies
　　　To blaze these last, and sware devoutly then,
　　　The first, thus matcht, were scarcely Gentlemen.

14 ALAS have I not paine enough my friend,
　　Upon whose breast a fiercer Gripe doth tire
　　Then did on him who first stale downe the fire,
While *Love* on me doth all his quiver spend,
But with your Rubarb words yow must contend
　　To grieve me worse, in saying that Desire
　　Doth plunge my wel-form'd soule even in the mire
Of sinfull thoughts, which do in ruine end?
　　If that be sinne which doth the maners frame,
Well staid with truth in word and faith of deed,
Readie of wit and fearing nought but shame:
If that be sinne which in fixt hearts doth breed
　　A loathing of all loose unchastitie,
　　Then Love is sinne, and let me sinfull be.

15 YOU that do search for everie purling spring,
　　Which from the ribs of old *Parnassus* flowes,
　　And everie floure, not sweet perhaps, which growes
Neare therabout, into your Poesie wring;
You that do Dictionarie's methode bring
　　Into your rimes, running in ratling rowes:
　　You that poore *Petrarch's* long deceased woes,
With new-borne sighes and denisend wit do sing;

8

You take wrong waies, those far-fet helpes be such,
    As do bewray a want of inward tuch:
And sure at length stolne goods do come to light.
    But if (both for your love and skill) your name
    You seeke to nurse at fullest breasts of Fame,
Stella behold, and then begin to endite.

6 IN nature apt to like when I did see
    Beauties, which were of manie Carrets fine,
    My boiling sprites did thither soone incline,
And, Love, I thought that I was full of thee:
But finding not those restlesse flames in me,
    Which others said did make their soules to pine:
    I thought those babes of some pinne's hurt did whine,
By my love judging what Love's paine might be.
    But while I thus with this yong Lyon plaid;
Mine eyes (shall I say curst or blest) beheld
Stella; now she is nam'd, need more be said?
In her sight I a lesson new have speld,
    I now have learn'd Love right, and learn'd even so,
    As who by being poisond doth poison know.

7 HIS mother deare *Cupid* offended late,
    Because that *Mars,* growne slacker in her love,
    With pricking shot he did not throughly move,
To keepe the pace of their first loving state.
The boy refusde for feare of *Marse's* hate,
    Who threatned stripes, if he his wrath did prove:
    But she in chafe him from her lap did shove,
Brake bow, brake shafts, while *Cupid* weeping sate:
    Till that his grandame *Nature* pittying it,
Of *Stella's* browes made him two better bowes,
And in her eyes of arrowes infinit.
O how for joy he leapes, ô how he crowes,
    And straight therewith, like wags new got to play,
    Fals to shrewd turnes, and I was in his way.

18
WITH what sharpe checkes I in my selfe am shent,
    When into Reason's audite I do go:
    And by just counts my selfe a banckrout know
Of all those goods, which heav'n to me hath lent:
Unable quite to pay even Nature's rent,
    Which unto it by birthright I do ow:
    And which is worse, no good excuse can show,
But that my wealth I have most idly spent.
    My youth doth waste, my knowledge brings forth toyes,
My wit doth strive those passions to defend,
Which for reward spoile it with vaine annoyes.
I see my course to lose my selfe doth bend:
    I see and yet no greater sorow take,
    Then that I lose no more for *Stella's* sake.

19
ON *Cupid's* bow how are my heart-strings bent,
    That see my wracke, and yet embrace the same?
    When most I glorie, then I feele most shame:
I willing run, yet while I run, repent.
My best wits still their owne disgrace invent:
    My verie inke turnes straight to *Stella's* name;
    And yet my words, as them my pen doth frame,
Avise themselves that they are vainely spent.
    For though she passe all things, yet what is all
That unto me, who fare like him that both
Lookes to the skies, and in a ditch doth fall?
O let me prop my mind, yet in his growth
    And not in Nature for best fruits unfit:
    'Scholler,' saith *Love,* 'bend hitherward your wit.'

20
FLIE, fly, my friends, I have my death wound; fly,
See there that boy, that murthring boy I say,
Who like a theefe, hid in darke bush doth ly,
Till bloudie bullet get him wrongfull pray.
    So Tyran he no fitter place could spie,
Nor so faire levell in so secret stay,
As that sweete blacke which vailes the heav'nly eye:
There himselfe with his shot he close doth lay.

10

Poore passenger, passe now thereby I did,
And staid pleasd with the prospect of the place,
While that blacke hue from me the bad guest hid:
But straight I saw motions of lightning' grace,
    And then descried the glistring of his dart:
    But ere I could flie thence, it piere'd my heart.

21   YOUR words my friend (right healthfull caustiks) blame
    My young mind marde, whom *Love* doth windlas so,
    That mine owne writings like bad servants show
My wits, quicke in vaine thoughts, in vertue lame:
That *Plato* I read for nought, but if he tame
    Such coltish gyres, that to my birth I owe
    Nobler desires, least else that friendly foe,
Great expectation, weare a traine of shame.
    For since mad March great promise made of me,
If now the May of my yeares much decline,
What can be hoped my harvest time will be?
Sure you say well, your wisdome's golden mine
    Dig deepe with learning's spade, now tell me this,
    Hath this world ought so faire as *Stella* is?

22   IN highest way of heav'n the Sunne did ride,
    Progressing then from faire twinnes' gold'n place:
    Having no scarfe of clowds before his face,
But shining forth of heate in his chiefe pride;
When some faire Ladies, by hard promise tied,
    On horsebacke met him in his furious race,
    Yet each prepar'd, with fanne's wel-shading grace,
From that foe's wounds their tender skinnes to hide.
Stella alone with face unarmed marcht,
    Either to do like him, which open shone,
    Or carelesse of the wealth because her owne:
Yet were the hid and meaner beauties parcht,
    Her daintiest bare went free; the cause was this,
    The Sunne which others burn'd, did her but kisse.

23   THE curious wits, seeing dull pensivenesse
      Bewray it selfe in my long setled eyes,
      Whence those same fumes of melancholy rise,
   With idle paines, and missing ayme, do guesse.
   Some that know how my spring I did addresse,
      Deeme that my Muse some fruit of knowledge plies:
      Others, because the Prince my service tries,
   Thinke that I thinke state errours to redresse.
      But harder Judges judge ambition's rage,
   Scourge of it selfe, still climing slipprie place,
   Holds my young braine captiv'd in golden cage.
   O fooles, or over-wise, alas the race
      Of all my thoughts hath neither stop nor start,
      But only *Stella's* eyes and *Stella's* hart.

24   RICH fooles there be, whose base and filthy hart
   Lies hatching still the goods wherein they flow:
   And damning their owne selves to *Tantal's* smart,
   Wealth breeding want, more blist, more wretched grow.
      Yet to those fooles heav'n such wit doth impart,
   As what their hands do hold, their heads do know,
   And knowing, love, and loving, lay apart
   As sacred things, far from all daunger's show.
      But that rich foole, who by blind Fortune's lot
   The richest gemme of Love and life enjoyes,
   And can with foule abuse such beauties blot;
   Let him, deprived of sweet but unfelt joyes,
      (Exil'd for ay from those high treasures, which
      He knowes not) grow in only follie rich.

25   THE wisest scholler of the wight most wise
   By *Phœbus'* doome, with sugred sentence sayes,
   That Vertue, if it once met with our eyes,
   Strange flames of *Love* it in our soules would raise;
      But for that man with paine this truth descries,
   While he each thing in sense's ballance wayes,
   And so nor will, nor can, behold those skies
   Which inward sunne to *Heroicke* minde displaies,

Vertue of late, with vertuous care to ster
Love of her selfe, takes *Stella's* shape, that she
To mortall eyes might sweetly shine in her.
It is most true, for since I her did see,
　　Vertue's great beautie in that face I prove,
　　And find th'effect, for I do burne in love.

26　THOUGH dustie wits dare scorne Astrologie,
And fooles can thinke those Lampes of purest light,
Whose numbers, wayes, greatnesse, eternitie,
Promising wonders, wonder to invite,
　　To have for no cause birthright in the skie,
　　But for to spangle the blacke weeds of night:
　　Or for some brawle, which in that chamber hie,
They should still daunce to please a gazer's sight.
　　For me, I do Nature unidle know,
And know great causes, great effects procure:
And know those Bodies high raigne on the low.
And if these rules did faile, proofe makes me sure,
　　Who oft fore-judge my after-following race,
　　By only those two starres in *Stella's* face.

27　BECAUSE I oft in darke abstracted guise,
　　Seeme most alone in greatest companie,
　　With dearth of words, or answers quite awrie,
To them that would make speech of speech arise,
They deeme, and of their doome the rumour flies,
　　That poison foule of bubling pride doth lie
　　So in my swelling breast that only I
Fawne on my self, and others to despise:
　　Yet pride I thinke doth not my soule possesse,
Which lookes too oft in his unflattring glasse:
But one worse fault, *Ambition,* I confesse,
That makes me oft my best friends overpasse,
　　Unseene, unheard, while thought to highest place
　　Bends all his powers, even unto *Stella's* grace.

28   YOU that with allegorie's curious frame,
      Of other's children changelings use to make,
      With me those paines for God's sake do not take:
   I list not dig so deepe for brasen fame.
   When I say *'Stella',* I do meane the same
      Princesse of Beautie, for whose only sake
      The raines of *Love* I love, though never slake,
   And joy therein, though Nations count it shame.
      I beg no subject to use eloquence,
   Nor in hid wayes to guide Philosophie:
   Looke at my hands for no such quintessence;
   But know that I in pure simplicitie,
      Breathe out the flames which burne within my heart,
      Love onely reading unto me this art.

29   LIKE some weake Lords, neighbord by mighty kings,
      To keepe themselves and their chiefe cities free,
      Do easly yeeld, that all their coasts may be
   Ready to store their campes of needfull things:
   So *Stella's* heart, finding what power *Love* brings,
      To keepe it selfe in life and liberty,
      Doth willing graunt, that in the frontiers he
   Use all to helpe his other conquerings:
   And thus her heart escapes, but thus her eyes
      Serve him with shot, her lips his heralds arre:
      Her breasts his tents, legs his triumphall carre:
   Her flesh his food, her skin his armour brave,
   And I, but for because my prospect lies
   Upon that coast, am giv'n up for a slave.

30   WHETHER the Turkish new-moone minded be
      To fill his hornes this yeare on Christian coast;
      How *Poles'* right king meanes, without leave of hoast,
   To warme with ill-made fire cold *Moscovy;*
   If French can yet three parts in one agree;
      What now the Dutch in their full diets boast;
      How *Holland* hearts, now so good townes be lost,
   Trust in the shade of pleasing *Orange* tree;

How *Ulster* likes of that same golden bit,
Wherewith my father once made it halfe tame;
If in the Scottishe Court be weltring yet;
These questions busie wits to me do frame;
  I, cumbred with good maners, answer do,
  But know not how, for still I thinke of you.

WITH how sad steps, ô Moone, thou climb'st the skies,
  How silently, and with how wanne a face,
  What, may it be that even in heav'nly place
That busie archer his sharpe arrowes tries?
Sure, if that long with *Love* acquainted eyes
  Can judge of *Love,* thou feel'st a Lover's case;
  I reade it in thy lookes, thy languisht grace,
To me that feele the like, thy state descries.
  Then ev'n of fellowship, ô Moone, tell me
Is constant *Love* deem'd there but want of wit?
Are Beauties there as proud as here they be?
Do they above love to be lov'd, and yet
  Those Lovers scorne whom that *Love* doth possesse?
  Do they call *Vertue* there ungratefulnesse?

MORPHEUS, the lively sonne of deadly sleepe,
  Witnesse of life to them that living die:
  A Prophet oft, and oft an historie,
A Poet eke, as humours fly or creepe,
Since thou in me so sure a power doest keepe,
  That never I with clos'd-up sense do lie,
  But by thy worke my *Stella* I descrie,
Teaching blind eyes both how to smile and weepe,
  Vouchsafe of all acquaintance this to tell,
Whence hast thou Ivorie, Rubies, pearle and gold,
To shew her skin, lips, teeth and head so well?
'Foole,' answers he, 'no *Indes* such treasures hold,
  But from thy heart, while my sire charmeth thee,
  Sweet *Stella's* image I do steale to mee.'

33 I MIGHT, unhappie word, ô me, I might,
    And then would not, or could not see my blisse:
    Till now, wrapt in a most infernall night,
    I find how heav'nly day wretch I did misse.
        Hart rent thy selfe, thou doest thy selfe but right,
    No lovely *Paris* made thy *Hellen* his:
    No force, no fraud, robd thee of thy delight,
    Nor Fortune of thy fortune author is:
        But to my selfe my selfe did give the blow,
    While too much wit (forsooth) so troubled me,
    That I respects for both our sakes must show:
    And yet could not by rising Morne foresee
        How faire a day was neare, ô punisht eyes,
        That I had bene more foolish or more wise.

34 COME let me write, 'And to what end?' To ease
        A burthned hart. 'How can words ease, which are
        The glasses of thy dayly vexing care?'
    Oft cruell fights well pictured forth do please.
    'Art not asham'd to publish thy disease?'
        Nay, that may breed my fame, it is so rare:
        'But will not wise men thinke thy words fond ware?'
    Then be they close, and so none shall displease.
        'What idler thing, then speake and not be hard?'
    What harder thing then smart, and not to speake?
    Peace, foolish wit, with wit my wit is mard.
    Thus write I while I doubt to write, and wreake
        My harmes on Ink's poore losse, perhaps some find
        Stella's great powrs, that so confuse my mind.

35 WHAT may words say, or what may words not say,
    Where truth it selfe must speake like flatterie?
    Within what bounds can one his liking stay,
    Where Nature doth with infinite agree?
        What *Nestor's* counsell can my flames alay,
    Since Reason's selfe doth blow the cole in me?
    And ah what hope, that hope should once see day,
    Where *Cupid* is sworne page to Chastity?

16

Honour is honour'd, that thou doest possesse
   Him as thy slave, and now long needy Fame
   Doth even grow rich, naming my *Stella's* name.
Wit learnes in thee perfection to expresse,
   Not thou by praise, but praise in thee is raisde:
   It is a praise to praise, when thou art praisde.

6   *STELLA* , whence doth this new assault arise,
A conquerd, yelden, ransackt heart to winne?
Whereto long since, through my long battred eyes,
Whole armies of thy beauties entred in.
   And there long since, *Love* thy Lieutenant lies,
My forces razde, thy banners raisd within:
Of conquest, do not these effects suffice,
But wilt new warre upon thine owne begin?
   With so sweete voice, and by sweete Nature so,
In sweetest strength, so sweetly skild withall,
In all sweete stratagems sweete Arte can show,
That not my soule, which at thy foot did fall,
   Long since forc'd by thy beames, but stone nor tree
   By Sence's priviledge, can scape from thee.

7   MY mouth doth water, and my breast doth swell,
   My tongue doth itch, my thoughts in labour be:
   Listen then Lordings with good eare to me,
For of my life I must a riddle tell.
Towardes *Aurora's* Court a Nymph doth dwell,
   Rich in all beauties which man's eye can see:
   Beauties so farre from reach of words, that we
Abase her praise, saying she doth excell:
   Rich in the treasure of deserv'd renowne,
Rich in the riches of a royall hart,
Rich in those gifts which give th'eternall crowne;
Who though most rich in these and everie part,
   Which make the patents of true worldly blisse,
   Hath no misfortune, but that Rich she is.

38   THIS night while sleepe begins with heavy wings
        To hatch mine eyes, and that unbitted thought
        Doth fall to stray, and my chiefe powres are brought
    To leave the scepter of all subject things,
    The first that straight my fancie's error brings
        Unto my mind, is *Stella's* image, wrought
        By *Love's* owne selfe, but with so curious drought,
    That she, me thinks, not onely shines but sings.
    I start, looke, hearke, but what in closde up sence
    Was held, in opend sense it flies away,
    Leaving me nought but wailing eloquence:
    I, seeing better sights in sight's decay,
        Cald it anew, and wooed sleepe againe:
        But him her host that unkind guest had slaine.

39   COME sleepe, ô sleepe, the certaine knot of peace,
    The baiting place of wit, the balme of woe,
    The poore man's wealth, the prisoner's release,
    Th'indifferent Judge betweene the high and low,
        With shield of proofe shield me from out the prease
    Of those fierce darts, dispaire at me doth throw:
    O make in me those civill warres to cease;
    I will good tribute pay if thou do so.
        Take thou of me smooth pillowes, sweetest bed,
    A chamber deafe to noise, and blind to light:
    A rosie garland, and a wearie hed:
    And if these things, as being thine by right,
        Move not thy heavy grace, thou shalt in me,
        Livelier then else-where, *Stella's* image see.

40   AS good to write as for to lie and grone.
        O *Stella* deare, how much thy power hath wrought,
        That hast my mind, none of the basest, brought
    My still kept course, while others sleepe, to mone.
    Alas, if from the height of Vertue's throne,
        Thou canst vouchsafe the influence of a thought
        Upon a wretch, that long thy grace hath sought;
    Weigh then how I by thee am overthrowne:

And then, thinke thus, although thy beautie be
Made manifest by such a victorie,
Yet noblest Conquerours do wreckes avoid.
Since then thou hast so farre subdued me,
That in my heart I offer still to thee,
O do not let thy Temple be destroyd.

1 HAVING this day my horse, my hand, my launce
Guided so well, that I obtain'd the prize,
Both by the judgement of the English eyes,
And of some sent from that sweet enemie *Fraunce;*
Horsemen my skill in horsmanship advaunce;
Towne-folkes my strength; a daintier judge applies
His praise to sleight, which from good use doth rise;
Some luckie wits impute it but to chaunce;
Others, because of both sides I do take
My bloud from them, who did excell in this,
Thinke Nature me a man of armes did make.
How farre they shoote awrie! the true cause is,
Stella lookt on, and from her heavenly face
Sent forth the beames, which made so faire my race.

2 O EYES, which do the Spheares of beautie move,
Whose beames be joyes, whose joyes all vertues be,
Who while they make *Love* conquer, conquer *Love,*
The schooles where *Venus* hath learn'd Chastitie.
O eyes, where humble lookes most glorious prove,
Only lov'd Tyrants, just in cruelty,
Do not, ô do not from poore me remove,
Keepe still my Zenith, ever shine on me.
For though I never see them, but straight wayes
My life forgets to nourish languisht sprites;
Yet still on me, ô eyes, dart downe your rayes:
And if from Majestie of sacred lights,
Oppressing mortall sense, my death proceed,
Wrackes Triumphs be, which *Love* (high set) doth breed.

43   FAIRE eyes, sweet lips, deare heart, that foolish I
Could hope by *Cupid's* helpe on you to pray;
Since to himselfe he doth your gifts apply,
As his maine force, choise sport, and easefull stay.

    For when he will see who dare him gainesay,
Then with those eyes he lookes, lo by and by
Each soule doth at *Love's* feet his weapons lay,
Glad if for her he give them leave to die.

    When he will play, then in her lips he is,
Where blushing red, that *Love's* selfe them doth love,
With either lip he doth the other kisse:
But when he will for quiet's sake remove

        From all the world, her heart is then his rome,
        Where well he knowes, no man to him can come.

44   MY words I know do well set forth my mind,
    My mind bemones his sense of inward smart;
    Such smart may pitie claime of any hart,
Her heart, sweete heart, is of no Tygre's kind:
And yet she heares, yet I no pitty find;
    But more I crie, lesse grace she doth impart,
    Alas, what cause is there so overthwart,
That Noblenesse it selfe makes thus unkind?
    I much do guesse, yet find no truth save this,
That when the breath of my complaints doth tuch
Those daintie dores unto the Court of blisse,
The heav'nly nature of that place is such,

        That once come there, the sobs of mine annoyes
        Are metamorphosd straight to tunes of joyes.

45   *STELLA* oft sees the verie face of wo
    Painted in my beclowded stormie face:
    But cannot skill to pitie my disgrace,
Not though thereof the cause her selfe she know:
Yet hearing late a fable, which did show
    Of Lovers never knowne, a grievous case,
    Pitie thereof gate in her breast such place
That, from that sea deriv'd, teares' spring did flow.

Alas, if Fancy drawne by imag'd things,
Though false, yet with free scope more grace doth breed
Then servant's wracke, where new doubts honor brings;
Then thinke my deare, that you in me do reed
    Of Lover's ruine some sad Tragedie:
    I am not I, pitie the tale of me.

6   I CURST thee oft, I pitie now thy case,
        Blind-hitting boy, since she that thee and me
        Rules with a becke, so tyrannizeth thee,
    That thou must want or food, or dwelling place.
    For she protests to banish thee her face,
        Her face? O *Love,* a Rogue thou then shouldst be,
        If *Love* learne not alone to love and see,
    Without desire to feed of further grace.
        Alas poore wag, that now a scholler art
    To such a schoole-mistresse, whose lessons new
    Thou needs must misse, and so thou needs must smart.
    Yet Deare, let me this pardon get of you,
        So long (though he from booke myche to desire)
        Till without fewell you can make hot fire.

7   WHAT, have I thus betrayed my libertie?
        Can those blacke beames such burning markes engrave
        In my free side? or am I borne a slave,
    Whose necke becomes such yoke of tyranny?
    Or want I sense to feele my miserie?
        Or sprite, disdaine of such disdaine to have?
        Who for long faith, tho dayly helpe I crave,
    May get no almes but scorne of beggerie.
        Vertue awake, Beautie but beautie is,
    I may, I must, I can, I will, I do
    Leave following that, which it is gaine to misse.
    Let her go. Soft, but here she comes. Go to,
        Unkind, I love you not: O me, that eye
        Doth make my heart give to my tongue the lie.

48   SOULE'S joy, bend not those morning starres from me,
        Where Vertue is made strong by Beautie's might,
        Where *Love* is chastnesse, Paine doth learne delight,
And Humblenesse growes one with Majestie.
What ever may ensue, ô let me be
        Copartner of the riches of that sight:
        Let not mine eyes be hel-driv'n from that light:
O looke, ô shine, ô let me die and see.
        For though I oft my selfe of them bemone,
        That through my heart their beamie darts be gone,
Whose curelesse wounds even now most freshly bleed:
        Yet since my death-wound is already got,
        Deare Killer, spare not thy sweet cruell shot:
A kind of grace it is to slay with speed.

49   I ON my horse, and *Love* on me doth trie
        Our horsmanships, while by strange worke I prove
        A horsman to my horse, a horse to *Love;*
And now man's wrongs in me, poore beast, descrie.
The raines wherewith my Rider doth me tie,
        Are humbled thoughts, which bit of Reverence move,
        Curb'd in with feare, but with guilt bosse above
Of Hope, which makes it seeme faire to the eye.
        The Wand is Will, thou Fancie Saddle art,
Girt fast by memorie, and while I spurre
My horse, he spurres with sharpe desire my hart:
He sits me fast, how ever I do sturre:
        And now hath made me to his hand so right,
        That in the Manage myselfe takes delight.

50   *STELLA*, the fulnesse of my thoughts of thee
Cannot be staid within my panting breast,
But they do swell and struggle forth of me,
Till that in words thy figure be exprest.
    And yet as soone as they so formed be,
According to my Lord *Love's* owne behest:
With sad eyes I their weake proportion see,
To portrait that which in this world is best.

So that I cannot chuse but write my mind,
And cannot chuse but put out what I write,
While those poore babes their death in birth do find:
And now my pen these lines had dashed quite,
   But that they stopt his furie from the same,
   Because their forefront bare sweet *Stella's* name.

51   PARDON mine eares, both I and they do pray,
      So may your tongue still fluently proceed,
      To them that do such entertainment need,
   So may you still have somewhat new to say.
   On silly me do not the burthen lay,
      Of all the grave conceits your braine doth breed;
      But find some *Hercules* to beare, in steed
   Of *Atlas* tyr'd, your wisedome's heav'nly sway.
      For me, while you discourse of courtly tides,
   Of cunningst fishers in most troubled streames,
   Of straying wayes, when valiant errour guides:
   Meane while my heart confers with *Stella's* beames,
      And is even irkt that so sweet Comedie,
      By such unsuted speech should hindred be.

52   A STRIFE is growne betweene *Vertue* and *Love,*
      While each pretends that *Stella* must be his:
      Her eyes, her lips, her all, saith *Love* do this,
   Since they do weare his badge, most firmely prove.
   But *Vertue* thus that title doth disprove,
      That *Stella* (ô deare name) that *Stella* is
      That vertuous soule, sure heire of heav'nly blisse:
   Not this faire outside, which our hearts doth move.
      And therefore, though her beautie and her grace
   Be *Love's* indeed, in *Stella's* selfe he may
   By no pretence claime any maner place.
   Well *Love,* since this demurre our sute doth stay,
      Let *Vertue* have that *Stella's* selfe; yet thus,
      That *Vertue* but that body graunt to us.

53   IN Martiall sports I had my cunning tride,
      And yet to breake more staves did me addresse:
      While with the people's shouts I must confesse,
    Youth, lucke, and praise, even fild my veines with pride.
    When *Cupid,* having me his slave describe
      In *Marse's* liverie, prauncing in the presse:
      'What now sir foole,' said he, 'I would no lesse,
    Looke here, I say.' I look'd, and *Stella* spide,
      Who hard by made a window send forth light.
    My heart then quak'd, then dazled were mine eyes,
    One hand forgott to rule, th'other to fight.
    Nor trumpets' sound I heard, nor friendly cries;
      My Foe came on, and beat the aire for me,
      Till that her blush taught me my shame to see.

54   BECAUSE I breathe not love to everie one,
      Nor do not use set colours for to weare,
      Nor nourish speciall lockes of vowed haire,
    Nor give each speech a full point of a grone,
    The courtly Nymphs, acquainted with the mone
      Of them, who in their lips *Love's* standerd beare;
      'What he?' say they of me, 'now I dare sweare,
    He cannot love: no, no, let him alone.'
      And thinke so still, so *Stella* know my mind,
    Professe in deed I do not *Cupid's* art;
    But you faire maides, at length this true shall find,
    That his right badge is but worne in the hart:
      Dumbe Swannes, not chatring Pies, do Lovers prove,
      They love indeed, who quake to say they love.

55   MUSES, I oft invoked your holy ayde,
      With choisest flowers my speech to engarland so;
      That it, despisde in true but naked shew,
    Might winne some grace in your sweet skill arraid.
    And oft whole troupes of saddest words I staid,
      Striving abroad a foraging to go,
      Untill by your inspiring I might know,
    How their blacke banner might be best displaid.

But now I meane no more your helpe to trie,
Nor other sugring of my speech to prove,
But on her name incessantly to crie:
For let me but name her whom I do love,
    So sweete sounds straight mine eare and heart do hit,
    That I well find no eloquence like it.

6 FY, schoole of Patience, Fy, your lesson is
    Far far too long to learne it without booke:
    What, a whole weeke without one peece of looke,
And thinke I should not your large precepts misse?
When I might reade those letters faire of blisse,
    Which in her face teach vertue, I could brooke
    Somewhat thy lead'n counsels, which I tooke
As of a friend that meant not much amisse:
    But now that I, alas, do want her sight,
What, dost thou thinke that I can ever take
In thy cold stuffe a flegmatike delight?
No Patience, if thou wilt my good, then make
    Her come, and heare with patience my desire,
    And then with patience bid me beare my fire.

7 WO, having made with many fights his owne
    Each sence of mine, each gift, each power of mind,
    Growne now his slaves, he forst them out to find
The thorowest words, fit for woe's selfe to grone,
Hoping that when they might find *Stella* alone,
    Before she could prepare to be unkind,
    Her soule, arm'd but with such a dainty rind,
Should soone be pierc'd with sharpnesse of the mone.
    She heard my plaints, and did not only heare,
But them (so sweete is she) most sweetly sing,
With that faire breast making woe's darknesse cleare:
A prety case! I hoped her to bring
    To feele my griefes, and she with face and voice
    So sweets my paines, that my paines me rejoyce.

58   DOUBT there hath bene, when with his golden chaine
          The Oratour so farre men's harts doth bind,
          That no pace else their guided steps can find,
      But as he them more short or slacke doth raine,
      Whether with words this soveraignty he gaine,
          Cloth'd with fine tropes, with strongest reasons lin'd,
          Or else pronouncing grace, wherewith his mind
      Prints his owne lively forme in rudest braine.
          Now judge by this: in piercing phrases late,
          Th' anatomy of all my woes I wrate,
      Stella's sweete breath the same to me did reed.
          O voice, ô face, maugre my speeche's might,
          Which wooed wo, most ravishing delight
      Even those sad words even in sad me did breed.

59   DEARE, why make you more of a dog then me?
          If he do love, I burne, I burne in love:
          If he waite well, I never thence would move:
      If he be faire, yet but a dog can be.
      Litle he is, so litle worth is he;
          He barks, my songs thine owne voyce oft doth prove:
          Bid'n, perhaps he fetcheth thee a glove,
      But I unbid, fetch even my soule to thee.
          Yet while I languish, him that bosome clips,
          That lap doth lap, nay lets, in spite of spite,
      This sowre-breath'd mate tast of those sugred lips.
          Alas, if you graunt only such delight
          To witlesse things, then *Love* I hope (since wit
      Becomes a clog) will soone ease me of it.

60   WHEN my good Angell guides me to the place,
          Where all my good I do in *Stella* see,
          That heav'n of joyes throwes onely downe on me
      Thundred disdaines and lightnings of disgrace:
      But when the ruggedst step of Fortune's race
          Makes me fall from her sight, then sweetly she
          With words, wherein the Muses' treasures be,
      Shewes love and pitie to my absent case.

Now I, wit-beaten long by hardest Fate,
So dull am, that I cannot looke into
The ground of this fierce *Love* and lovely hate:
Then some good body tell me how I do,
    Whose presence,absence, absence presence is;
    Blist in my curse, and cursed in my blisse.

OFT with true sighes, oft with uncalled teares,
Now with slow words, now with dumbe eloquence
I *Stella's* eyes assayll, invade her eares;
But this at last is her sweet breath'd defence:
    That who indeed infelt affection beares,
So captives to his Saint both soule and sence,
That wholly hers, all selfnesse he forbeares,
Thence his desires he learnes, his live's course thence.
    Now since her chast mind hates this love in me,
    With chastned mind, I straight must shew that she
Shall quickly me from what she hates remove.
    O Doctor *Cupid,* thou for me reply,
    Driv'n else to graunt by Angel's sophistrie,
That I love not, without I leave to love.

LATE tyr'd with wo, even ready for to pine
With rage of *Love,* I cald my Love unkind;
She in whose eyes *Love,* though unfelt, doth shine,
Sweet said that I true love in her should find.
    I joyed, but straight thus watred was my wine,
That love she did, but loved a Love not blind,
Which would not let me, whom she loved, decline
From nobler course, fit for my birth and mind: —
    And therefore by her Love's authority,
    Willd me these tempests of vaine love to flie,
And anchor fast my selfe on *Vertue's* shore.
    Alas, if this the only mettall be
    Of *Love,* new-coind to helpe my beggery,
Deare, love me not, that you may love me more.

63 O GRAMMER rules, ô now your vertues show;
   So children still reade you with awfull eyes,
   As my young Dove may in your precepts wise
Her graunt to me, by her owne vertue know.
For late with heart most high, with eyes most low,
   I crav'd the thing which ever she denies:
   She lightning *Love,* displaying *Venus'* skies,
Least once should not be heard, twise said, No, No.
   Sing then my Muse, now *Io Pean* sing,
   Heav'ns envy not at my high triumphing:
But Grammer's force with sweet successe confirme,
   For Grammer sayes (ô this deare *Stella* weighe,)
   For Grammer sayes (to Grammer who sayes nay)
That in one speech two Negatives affirme.

First song

DOUBT you to whom my Muse these notes entendeth,
Which now my breast orecharg'd to Musicke lendeth?
To you, to you, all song of praise is due,
Only in you my song begins and endeth.

Who hath the eyes which marrie state with pleasure, [5]
Who keepes the key of Nature's chiefest treasure?
To you, to you, all song of praise is due,
Only for you the heav'n forgate all measure.

Who hath the lips, where wit in fairenesse raigneth,
Who womankind at once both deckes and stayneth? [10]
To you, to you, all song of praise is due,
Onely by you *Cupid* his crowne maintaineth.

Who hath the feet, whose step all sweetnesse planteth,
Who else for whom *Fame* worthy trumpets wanteth?
To you, to you, all song of praise is due, [15]
Onely to you her Scepter *Venus* granteth.

Who hath the breast, whose milke doth passions nourish,
Whose grace is such, that when it chides doth cherish?

28

To you, to you, all song of praise is due,
Onelie through you the tree of life doth flourish.   [20]

Who hath the hand which without stroke subdueth,
Who long dead beautie with increase reneweth?
To you, to you, all song of praise is due,
Onely at you all envie hopelesse rueth.

Who hath the haire which, loosest, fastest tieth,   [25]
Who makes a man live then glad when he dieth?
To you, to you, all song of praise is due:
Only of you the flatterer never lieth.

Who hath the voyce, which soule from sences sunders,
Whose force but yours the bolts of beautie thunders?   [30]
To you, to you, all song of praise is due:
Only with you not miracles are wonders.

Doubt you to whom my Muse these notes intendeth,
Which now my breast orecharg'd to Musicke lendeth?
To you, to you, all song of praise is due: [35]
Only in you my song begins and endeth.

NO more, my deare, no more these counsels trie,
    O give my passions leave to run their race:
    Let Fortune lay on me her worst disgrace,
Let folke orecharg'd with braine against me crie,
Let clouds bedimme my face, breake in mine eye,
    Let me no steps but of lost labour trace,
    Let all the earth with scorne recount my case,
But do not will me from my *Love* to flie.
    I do not envie *Aristotle's* wit,
Nor do aspire to *Cæsar's* bleeding fame,
Nor ought do care, though some above me sit,
Nor hope, nor wishe another course to frame,
    But that which once may win thy cruell hart:
    Thou art my Wit, and thou my Vertue art.

65   LOVE by sure proofe I may call thee unkind,
That giv'st no better eare to my just cries:
Thou whom to me such my good turnes should bind,
As I may well recount, but none can prize:
     For when, nak'd boy, thou couldst no harbour find
In this old world, growne now so too too wise:
I lodg'd thee in my heart, and being blind
By Nature borne, I gave to thee mine eyes.
     Mine eyes, my light, my heart, my life, alas,
If so great services may scorned be:
Yet let this thought thy Tygrish courage passe:
That I perhaps am somewhat kinne to thee;
     Since in thine armes, if learnd fame truth hath spread,
     Thou bear'st the arrow, I the arrow head.

66   AND do I see some cause a hope to feede,
Or doth the tedious burd'n of long wo
In weakened minds, quicke apprehending breed,
Of everie image, which may comfort show?
     I cannot brag of word, much lesse of deed,
Fortune wheeles still with me in one sort slow,
My wealth no more, and no whit lesse my need,
Desire still on the stilts of feare doth go.
     And yet amid all feares a hope there is
Stolne to my heart, since last faire night, nay day,
Stella's eyes sent to me the beames of blisse,
Looking on me, while I lookt other way:
     But when mine eyes backe to their heav'n did move,
     They fled with blush, which guiltie seem'd of love.

67   HOPE, art thou true, or doest thou flatter me?
     Doth *Stella* now begin with piteous eye,
     The ruines of her conquest to espie:
Will she take time, before all wracked be?
Her eye's-speech is translated thus by thee:
     But failst thou not in phrase so heav'nly hie?
     Looke on againe, the faire text better trie:
What blushing notes doest thou in margine see?

What sighes stolne out, or kild before full borne?
Hast thou found such and such like arguments?
Or art thou else to comfort me forsworne?
Well, how so thou interpret the contents,
    I am resolv'd thy errour to maintaine,
    Rather then by more truth to get more paine.

STELLA, the onely Planet of my light,
    Light of my life, and life of my desire,
    Chiefe good, whereto my hope doth only aspire,
World of my wealth, and heav'n of my delight.
Why doest thou spend the treasures of thy sprite,
    With voice more fit to wed *Amphion's* lyre,
    Seeking to quench in me the noble fire,
Fed by thy worth, and kindled by thy sight?
    And all in vaine, for while thy breath most sweet,
With choisest words, thy words with reasons rare,
Thy reasons firmly set on *Vertue's* feet,
Labour to kill in me this killing care:
    O think I then, what paradise of joy
    It is, so faire a Vertue to enjoy.

O JOY, too high for my low stile to show:
    O blisse, fit for a nobler state then me:
    Envie, put out thine eyes, least thou do see
What Oceans of delight in me do flow.
My friend, that oft saw through all maskes my wo,
    Come, come, and let me powre my selfe on thee;
    Gone is the winter of my miserie,
My spring appeares, ô see what here doth grow.
    For *Stella* hath with words where faith doth shine,
Of her high heart giv'n me the monarchie:
I, I, ô I may say, that she is mine.
And though she give but thus conditionly
    This realme of blisse, while vertuous course I take,
    No kings be crown'd but they some covenants make.

31

70   MY Muse may well grudge at my heav'nly joy,
If still I force her in sad rimes to creepe:
She oft hath drunke my teares, now hopes to enjoy
Nectar of Mirth, since I *Jove's* cup do keepe.
  Sonets be not bound prentise to annoy:
Trebles sing high, as well as bases deepe:
Griefe but *Love's* winter liverie is, the Boy
Hath cheekes to smile, as well as eyes to weepe.
  Come then my Muse, shew thou height of delight
In well raisde notes, my pen the best it may
Shall paint out joy, though but in blacke and white.
Cease eager Muse, peace pen, for my sake stay,
  I give you here my hand for truth of this,
  Wise silence is best musicke unto blisse.

71   WHO will in fairest booke of Nature know,
  How Vertue may best lodg'd in beautie be,
  Let him but learne of *Love* to reade in thee,
Stella, those faire lines, which true goodnesse show.
There shall he find all vices' overthrow,
  Not by rude force, but sweetest soveraigntie
  Of reason, from whose light those night-birds flie;
That inward sunne in thine eyes shineth so.
  And not content to be Perfection's heire
Thy selfe, doest strive all minds that way to move,
Who marke in thee what is in thee most faire.
So while thy beautie drawes the heart to love,
  As fast thy Vertue bends that love to good:
  'But ah,' Desire still cries, 'give me some food.'

72   DESIRE, though thou my old companion art,
  And oft so clings to my pure Love, that I
  One from the other scarcely can descrie,
While each doth blow the fier of my hart;

Now from thy fellowship I needs must part,
　　Venus is taught with *Dian's* wings to flie:
　　I must no more in thy sweet passions lie;
Vertue's gold now must head my *Cupid's* dart.
　　Service and Honor, wonder with delight,
Feare to offend, will worthie to appeare,
Care shining in mine eyes, faith in my sprite,
These things are left me by my only Deare;
　　　　But thou Desire, because thou wouldst have all,
　　　　Now banisht art, but yet alas how shall?

Second song

　　HAVE I caught my heav'nly jewell,
　　Teaching sleepe most faire to be?
　　Now will I teach her that she,
　　When she wakes, is too too cruell.

　　Since sweet sleep her eyes hath charmed,　　[5]
　　The two only darts of *Love*:
　　Now will I with that boy prove
　　Some play, while he is disarmed.

　　Her tongue waking still refuseth,
　　Giving frankly niggard No:　　[10]
　　Now will I attempt to know,
　　What No her tongue sleeping useth.

　　See the hand which waking gardeth,
　　Sleeping, grants a free resort:
　　Now will I invade the fort;　　[15]
　　Cowards *Love* with losse rewardeth.

　　But ô foole, thinke of the danger,
　　Of her just and high disdaine:
　　Now will I alas refraine,
　　Love feares nothing else but anger.　　[20]

Yet those lips so sweetly swelling,
Do invite a stealing kisse:
Now will I but venture this,
Who will read must first learne spelling.

Oh sweet kisse, but ah she is waking, [25]
Lowring beautie chastens me:
Now will I away hence flee:
Foole, more foole, for no more taking.

73   *LOVE* still a boy, and oft a wanton is,
School'd onely by his mother's tender eye:
What wonder then if he his lesson misse,
When for so soft a rod deare play he trie?
     And yet my Starre, because a sugred kisse
In sport I suckt, while she asleepe did lie,
Doth lowre, nay, chide; nay, threat for only this:
Sweet, it was saucie *Love,* not humble I.
     But no scuse serves, she makes her wrath appeare
     In Beautie's throne, see now who dares come neare
Those scarlet judges, threatning bloudy paine?
     O heav'nly foole, thy most kisse-worthie face,
     Anger invests with such a lovely grace,
That Anger' selfe I needs must kisse againe.

74   I NEVER dranke of *Aganippe* well,
Nor ever did in shade of *Tempe* sit:
And Muses scorne with vulgar braines to dwell,
Poore Layman I, for sacred rites unfit.
     Some do I heare of Poets' furie tell,
But (God wot) wot not what they meane by it:
And this I sweare by blackest brooke of hell,
I am no pick-purse of another's wit.

How falles it then, that with so smooth an ease
My thoughts I speake, and what I speake doth flow
In verse, and that my verse best wits doth please?
Guesse we the cause: 'What, is it thus?' Fie no:
    'Or so?' Much lesse: 'How then?' Sure thus it is:
    My lips are sweet, inspired with *Stella's* kisse.

O F all the kings that ever here did raigne,
Edward named fourth, as first in praise I name,
Not for his faire outside, nor well lined braine,
Although lesse gifts impe feathers oft on Fame,
    Nor that he could young-wise, wise-valiant frame
His Sire's revenge, joyn'd with a kingdome's gaine:
And gain'd by *Mars,* could yet mad *Mars* so tame,
That Ballance weigh'd what sword did late obtaine,
    Nor that he made the Flouredeluce so fraid,
Though strongly hedg'd of bloudy Lyon's pawes,
That wittie *Lewis* to him a tribute paid.
Nor this, nor that, nor any such small cause,
    But only for this worthy knight durst prove
    To lose his Crowne, rather then faile his Love.

S H E comes, and streight therewith her shining twins do move
    Their rayes to me, who in her tedious absence lay
    Benighted in cold wo, but now appeares my day,
The onely light of joy, the onely warmth of *Love.*
She comes with light and warmth, which like *Aurora* prove
    Of gentle force, so that mine eyes dare gladly play
    With such a rosie morne, whose beames most freshly gay
Scortch not, but onely do darke chilling sprites remove.
    But lo, while I do speake, it groweth noone with me,
Her flamie glistring lights increase with time and place;
My heart cries 'ah', it burnes, mine eyes now dazled be:
No wind, no shade can coole, what helpe then in my case,
    But with short breath, long lookes, staid feet and walking hed,
    Pray that my sunne go downe with meeker beames to bed.

77 THOSE lookes, whose beames be joy, whose motion is delight,
That face, whose lecture shewes what perfect beautie is:
That presence, which doth give darke hearts a living light:
That grace, which *Venus* weepes that she her selfe doth misse:
  That hand, which without touch holds more then *Atlas* might;
Those lips, which make death's pay a meane price for a kisse:
That skin, whose passe-praise hue scorns this poore terme of white:
Those words, which do sublime the quintessence of blisse:
  That voyce, which makes the soule plant himselfe in the eares:
That conversation sweet, where such high comforts be,
As consterd in true speech, the name of heav'n it beares,
Makes me in my best thoughts and quietst judgement see,
  That in no more but these I might be fully blest:
  Yet ah, my Mayd'n Muse doth blush to tell the best.

78 O HOW the pleasant aires of true love be
  Infected by those vapours, which arise
  From out that noysome gulfe, which gaping lies
Betweene the jawes of hellish Jealousie.
A monster, other's harme, selfe-miserie,
  Beautie's plague, Vertue's scourge, succour of lies:
  Who his owne joy to his owne hurt applies,
And onely cherish doth with injurie.
  Who since he hath, by Nature's speciall grace,
  So piercing pawes, as spoyle when they embrace,
So nimble feet as stirre still, though on thornes:
  So manie eyes ay seeking their owne woe,
  So ample eares as never good newes know:
Is it not evill that such a Devill wants hornes?

79 SWEET kisse, thy sweets I faine would sweetly endite,
  Which even of sweetnesse sweetest sweetner art:
  Pleasingst consort, where each sence holds a part,
Which, coupling Doves, guides *Venus'* chariot right.
Best charge, and bravest retrait in *Cupid's* fight,
  A double key, which opens to the heart,
  Most rich, when most his riches it impart:
Neast of young joyes, schoolmaster of delight,

36

Teaching the meane, at once to take and give
The friendly fray, where blowes both wound and heale,
The prettie death, while each in other live.
Poore hope's first wealth, ostage of promist weale,
    Breakefast of *Love,* but lo, lo, where she is,
    Cease we to praise, now pray we for a kisse.

SWEET swelling lip, well maist thou swell in pride,
    Since best wits thinke it wit thee to admire;
    Nature's praise, Vertue's stall, *Cupid's* cold fire,
Whence words, not words, but heav'nly graces slide.
The new *Pernassus,* where the Muses bide,
    Sweetner of musicke, wisedome's beautifier:
    Breather of life, and fastner of desire,
Where Beautie's blush in Honour's graine is dide.
    Thus much my heart compeld my mouth to say,
    But now spite of my heart my mouth will stay,
Loathing all lies, doubting this Flatterie is:
    And no spurre can his resty race renew,
    Without how farre this praise is short of you,
Sweet lip, you teach my mouth with one sweet kisse.

O KISSE, which doest those ruddie gemmes impart,
Or gemmes, or frutes of new-found *Paradise,*
Breathing all blisse and sweetning to the heart,
Teaching dumbe lips a nobler exercise.
    O kisse, which soules, even soules together ties
By linkes of *Love,* and only Nature's art:
How faine would I paint thee to all men's eyes,
Or of thy gifts at least shade out some part.
    But she forbids, with blushing words, she sayes,
    She builds her fame on higher seated praise:
But my heart burnes, I cannot silent be.
    Then since (deare life) you faine would have me peace,
    And I, mad with delight, want wit to cease,
Stop you my mouth with still still kissing me.

82   NYMPH of the gard'n, where all beauties be:
        Beauties which do in excellencie passe
        His who till death lookt in a watrie glasse,
    Or hers whom naked the *Trojan* boy did see.
    Sweet gard'n Nymph, which keepes the Cherrie tree,
        Whose fruit doth farre th'*Esperian* tast surpasse:
        Most sweet-faire, most faire-sweet, do not alas,
    From comming neare those Cherries banish me:
        For though full of desire, emptie of wit,
    Admitted late by your best-graced grace,
    I caught at one of them a hungrie bit;
    Pardon that fault, once more graunt me the place,
        And I do sweare even by the same delight,
        I will but kisse, I never more will bite.

83   GOOD brother *Philip,* I have borne you long,
        I was content you should in favour creepe,
        While craftily you seem'd your cut to keepe,
    As though that faire soft hand did you great wrong.
    I bare (with Envie) yet I bare your song,
        When in her necke you did *Love* ditties peepe;
        Nay, more foole I, oft suffered you to sleepe
    In Lillies' neast, where *Love's* selfe lies along.
        What, doth high place ambitious thoughts augment?
    Is sawcinesse reward of curtesie?
    Cannot such grace your silly selfe content,
    But you must needs with those lips billing be?
        And through those lips drinke Nectar from that toong;
        Leave that sir *Phip,* least off your necke be wroong.

Third song

IF *Orpheus'* voyce had force to breathe such musicke's love
Through pores of sencelesse trees, as it could make them move:
If stones good measure daunc'd, the *Theban* walles to build,
To cadence of the tunes, which *Amphyon's* lyre did yeeld,
More cause a like effect at leastwise bringeth: [5]
O stones, ô trees, learne hearing, *Stella* singeth.

If Love might sweet'n so a boy of shepheard' brood,
To make a Lyzard dull to taste Love's daintie food:
If Eagle fierce could so in *Grecian* Mayd delight,
As his light was her eyes, her death his endlesse night: [10]
Earth gave that Love, heav'n I trow Love refineth:
O birds, ô beasts, looke Love, lo, *Stella* shineth.

The birds, beasts, stones and trees feele this, and feeling *Love:*
And if the trees, nor stones stirre not the same to prove,
Nor beasts, nor birds do come unto this blessed gaze,   [15]
Know, that small Love is quicke, and great Love doth amaze:
They are amaz'd, but you with reason armed,
O eyes, ô eares of men, how are you charmed!

4   HIGHWAY since you my chiefe *Pernassus* be,
        And that my Muse to some eares not unsweet,
        Tempers her words to trampling horses feet,
    More oft then to a chamber melodie;
    Now blessed you, beare onward blessed me
        To her, where I my heart safeliest shall meet.
        My Muse and I must you of dutie greet
    With thankes and wishes, wishing thankfully.
        Be you still faire, honourd by publike heed,
    By no encrochment wrongd, nor time forgot:
    Nor blam'd for bloud, nor sham'd for sinfull deed.
    And that you know, I envy you no lot
        Of highest wish, I wish you so much blisse,
        Hundreds of yeares you *Stella's* feet may kisse.

5   I SEE the house, my heart thy selfe containe,
        Beware full sailes drowne not thy tottring barge:
        Least joy, by Nature apt sprites to enlarge,
    Thee to thy wracke beyond thy limits straine.
    Nor do like Lords, whose weake confused braine,
        Not pointing to fit folkes each undercharge,
        While everie office themselves will discharge,
    With doing all, leave nothing done but paine.

But give apt servants their due place, let eyes
See Beautie's totall summe summ'd in her face:
Let eares heare speech, which wit to wonder ties,
Let breath sucke up those sweetes, let armes embrace
    The globe of weale, lips *Love's* indentures make:
    Thou but of all the kingly Tribute take.

Fourth song

ONELY joy, now here you are,
Fit to heare and ease my care:
Let my whispering voyce obtaine,
Sweete reward for sharpest paine:
Take me to thee, and thee to me.   [5]
'No, no, no, no, my Deare, let be.'

Night hath closd all in her cloke,
Twinckling starres Love-thoughts provoke:
Danger hence good care doth keepe,
Jealousie it selfe doth sleepe: [10]
Take me to thee, and thee to me.
'No, no, no, no, my Deare, let be.'

Better place no wit can find,
Cupid's yoke to loose or bind:
These sweet flowers on fine bed too,   [15]
Us in their best language woo:
Take me to thee, and thee to me.
'No, no, no, no, my Deare, let be.'

This small light the Moone bestowes,
Serves thy beames but to disclose,   [20]
So to raise my hap more hie;
Feare not else, none can us spie:
Take me to thee, and thee to me.
'No, no, no, no, my Deare, let be.'

That you heard was but a Mouse, [25]
Dumbe sleepe holdeth all the house:
Yet a sleepe, me thinkes they say,
Yong folkes, take time while you may:
Take me to thee, and thee to me.
'No, no, no, no, my Deare, let be.' [30]

Niggard Time threats, if we misse
This large offer of our blisse,
Long stay ere he graunt the same:
Sweet then, while each thing doth frame:
Take me to thee, and thee to me. [35]
'No, no, no, no, my Deare, let be.'

Your faire mother is a bed,
Candles out, and curtaines spread:
She thinkes you do letters write:
Write, but first let me endite: [40]
Take me to thee, and thee to me.
'No, no, no, no, my Deare, let be.'

Sweet alas, why strive you thus?
Concord better fitteth us:
Leave to *Mars* the force of hands, [45]
Your power in your beautie stands:
Take me to thee, and thee to me.
'No, no, no, no, my Deare, let be.'

Wo to me, and do you sweare
Me to hate? But I forbeare, [50]
Cursed be my destines all,
That brought me so high to fall:
Soone with my death I will please thee.
'No, no, no, no, my Deare, let be.'

86   ALAS, whence came this change of lookes? If I
      Have chang'd desert, let mine owne conscience be
      A still felt plague, to selfe condemning me:
    Let wo gripe on my heart, shame loade mine eye.
    But if all faith, like spotlesse Ermine ly
      Safe in my soule, which only doth to thee
      (As his sole object of felicitie)
    With wings of *Love* in aire of wonder flie,
      O ease your hand, treate not so hard your slave:
    In justice paines come not till faults do call;
    Or if I needs (sweet Judge) must torments have,
    Use something else to chast'n me withall,
      Then those blest eyes, where all my hopes do dwell,
      No doome should make one's heav'n become his hell.

Fift song

WHILE favour fed my hope, delight with hope was brought,
Thought waited on delight, and speech did follow thought:
Then grew my tongue and pen records unto thy glory:
I thought all words were lost, that were not spent of thee:
I thought each place was darke but where thy lights would be, [4]
And all eares worse then deafe, that heard not out thy storie.

I said, thou wert most faire, and so indeed thou art:
I said, thou wert most sweet, sweet poison to my heart:
I said, my soule was thine (ô that I then had lyed)
I said, thine eyes were starres, thy breasts the milk'n way,   [10]
Thy fingers *Cupid's* shafts, thy voyce the Angels' lay:
And all I said so well, as no man it denied.

But now that hope is lost, unkindnesse kils delight,
Yet thought and speech do live, though metamorphosd quite:
For rage now rules the reynes, which guided were by Pleasure. [16]
I thinke now of thy faults, who late thought of thy praise,
That speech falles now to blame, which did thy honour raise,
The same key op'n can, which can locke up a treasure.

Thou then whom partiall heavens conspir'd in one to frame,
The proofe of Beautie's worth, th'enheritrix of fame,   [20]
The mansion seat of blisse, and just excuse of Lovers;
See now those feathers pluckt, wherewith thou flewst most high:
See what clouds of reproch shall darke thy honour's skie,
Whose owne fault casts him downe, hardly high seat recovers.

And ô my Muse, though oft you luld her in your lap,   [25]
And then, a heav'nly child, gave her Ambrosian pap:
And to that braine of hers your hidnest gifts infused,
Since she disdaining me, doth you in me disdaine:
Suffer not her to laugh, while both we suffer paine:
Princes in subjects wrongd, must deeme themselves abused.   [30]

Your Client poore my selfe, shall *Stella* handle so?
Revenge, revenge, my Muse, Defiance' trumpet blow:
Threat'n what may be done, yet do more then you threat'n.
Ah, my sute granted is, I feele my breast doth swell:
Now child, a lesson new you shall begin to spell: [35]
Sweet babes must babies have, but shrewd gyrles must be beat'n.

Thinke now no more to heare of warme fine odourd snow,
Nor blushing Lillies, nor pearles' ruby-hidden row,
Nor of that golden sea, whose waves in curles are brok'n:
But of thy soule, so fraught with such ungratefulnesse,   [40]
As where thou soone mightst helpe, most faith dost most oppresse,
Ungratefull who is cald, the worst of evils is spok'n.

Yet worse then worst, I say thou art a theefe, a theefe?
Now God forbid. A theefe, and of worst theeves the cheefe:
Theeves steal for need, and steale but goods, which paine recovers,
But thou rich in all joyes, doest rob my joyes from me,   [46]
Which cannot be restor'd by time nor industrie:
Of foes the spoile is evill, far worse of constant lovers.

Yet gentle English theeves do rob, but will not slay;
Thou English murdring theefe, wilt have harts for thy pray: [50]
The name of murdrer now on thy faire forehead sitteth:
And even while I do speake, my death wounds bleeding be:
Which (I protest) proceed from only Cruell thee,
Who may and will not save, murder in truth committeth.

43

But murder, private fault, seemes but a toy to thee,   [55]
I lay then to thy charge unjustest Tyrannie,
If Rule by force without all claime a Tyran showeth,
For thou doest lord my heart, who am not borne thy slave,
And which is worse, makes me most guiltlesse torments have,
A rightfull Prince by unright deeds a Tyran groweth.   [60]

Lo you grow proud with this, for tyrans make folke bow:
Of foule rebellion then I do appeach thee now;
Rebell by Nature's law, Rebell by law of reason,
Thou, sweetest subject, wert borne in the realme of Love,
And yet against thy Prince thy force dost dayly prove: [65]
No vertue merits praise, once toucht with blot of Treason.

But valiant Rebels oft in fooles' mouthes purchase fame:
I now then staine thy white with vagabunding shame,
Both Rebell to the Sonne, and Vagrant from the mother;
For wearing *Venus'* badge, in every part of thee,   [70]
Unto *Dianae's* traine thou runaway didst flee:
Who faileth one, is false, though trusty to another.

What, is not this enough? nay farre worse commeth here;
A witch I say thou art, though thou so faire appeare;
For I protest, my sight never thy face enjoyeth,   [75]
But I in me am chang'd, I am alive and dead:
My feete are turn'd to rootes, my hart becommeth lead,
No witchcraft is so evill, as which man's mind destroyeth.

Yet witches may repent, thou art far worse then they,
Alas, that I am forst such evill of thee to say,   [80]
I say thou art a Devill, though clothd in Angel's shining:
For thy face tempts my soule to leave the heav'n for thee,
And thy words of refuse, do powre even hell on mee:
Who tempt, and tempted plague, are Devils in true defining.

You then ungratefull thiefe, you murdring Tyran you,   [85]
You Rebell run away, to Lord and Lady untrue,
You witch, you Divill, (alas) you still of me beloved,
You see what I can say; mend yet your froward mind,
And such skill in my Muse you reconcil'd shall find,
That all these cruell words your praises shall be proved.   [90]

Sixt song

O YOU that heare this voice,
O you that see this face,
Say whether of the choice
Deserves the former place:
Feare not to judge this bate,   [5]
For it is void of hate.

This side doth beauty take,
For that doth Musike speake,
Fit oratours to make
The strongest judgements weake: [10]
The barre to plead their right,
Is only true delight.

Thus doth the voice and face,
These gentle Lawyers wage,
Like loving brothers' case   [15]
For father's heritage,
That each, while each contends,
It selfe to other lends.

For beautie beautifies,
With heavenly hew and grace,   [20]
The heavenly harmonies;
And in this faultlesse face,
The perfect beauties be
A perfect harmony.

Musicke more loftly swels   [25]
In speeches nobly placed:
Beauty as farre excels,
In action aptly graced:
A friend each party drawes,
To countenance his cause: [30]

Love more affected seemes
To beautie's lovely light,
And wonder more esteemes

45

Of Musick's wondrous might:
But both to both so bent, [35]
As both in both are spent.

Musike doth witnesse call
The eare, his truth to trie:
Beauty brings to the hall,
The judgement of the eye, [40]
Both in their objects such,
As no exceptions tutch.

The common sence, which might
Be Arbiter of this,
To be forsooth upright, [45]
To both sides partiall is:
He layes on this chiefe praise,
Chiefe praise on that he laies.

Then reason, Princesse hy,
Whose throne is in the mind, [50]
Which Musicke can in sky
And hidden beauties find,
Say whether thou wilt crowne,
With limitlesse renowne.

Seventh song

WHOSE senses in so evill consort, their stepdame Nature laies,
That ravishing delight in them most sweete tunes do not raise;
Or if they do delight therein, yet are so cloyed with wit,
As with sententious lips to set a title vaine on it: [4]
O let them heare these sacred tunes, and learne in wonder's schooles,
To be (in things past bounds of wit) fooles, if they be not fooles.

Who have so leaden eyes, as not to see sweet beautie's show,
Or seeing, have so wodden wits, as not that worth to know;
Or knowing, have so muddy minds, as not to be in love;
Or loving, have so frothy thoughts, as easly thence to move: [10]
O let them see these heavenly beames, and in faire letters reede
A lesson fit, both sight and skill, love and firme love to breede.

Heare then, but then with wonder heare; see but adoring see,
No mortall gifts, no earthly fruites, now here descended be:
See, do you see this face? a face? nay image of the skies,   [15]
Of which the two life-giving lights are figured in her eyes:
Heare you this soule-invading voice, and count it but a voice?
The very essence of their tunes, when Angels do rejoyce.

Eighth song

IN a grove most rich of shade,
Where birds wanton musicke made,
May then yong his pide weedes showing,
New perfumed with flowers fresh growing,

Astrophil with *Stella* sweete,   [5]
Did for mutuall comfort meete,
Both within themselves oppressed,
But each in the other blessed.

Him great harmes had taught much care,
Her faire necke a foule yoke bare,   [10]
But her sight his cares did banish,
In his sight her yoke did vanish.

Wept they had, alas the while,
But now teares themselves did smile,
While their eyes by love directed,   [15]
Enterchangeably reflected.

Sigh they did, but now betwixt
Sighs of woes were glad sighs mixt,
With armes crost, yet testifying
Restlesse rest, and living dying.   [20]

Their eares hungry of each word,
Which the deere tongue would afford,
But their tongues restraind from walking,
Till their harts had ended talking.

But when their tongues could not speake,   [25]
Love it selfe did silence breake;

Love did set his lips asunder,
Thus to speake in love and wonder:

'*Stella* soveraigne of my joy,
Faire triumpher of annoy,   [30]
Stella starre of heavenly fier,
Stella loadstar of desier.

'*Stella,* in whose shining eyes,
Are the lights of *Cupid's* skies,
Whose beames, where they once are darted,   [35]
Love therewith is streight imparted.

'*Stella,* whose voice when it speakes,
Senses all asunder breakes;
Stella, whose voice when it singeth,
Angels to acquaintance bringeth.   [40]

'*Stella,* in whose body is
Writ each character of blisse,
Whose face all, all beauty passeth,
Save thy mind which yet surpasseth.

'Graunt, ô graunt, but speech alas,   [45]
Failes me fearing on to passe,
Graunt, ô me, what am I saying?
But no fault there is in praying.

'Graunt, ô deere, on knees I pray,
(Knees on ground he then did stay)   [50]
That not I, but since I love you,
Time and place for me may move you.

'Never season was more fit,
Never roome more apt for it;
Smiling ayre allowes my reason,   [55]
These birds sing: "Now use the season."

'This small wind which so sweete is,
See how it the leaves doth kisse,
Ech tree in his best attiring,
Sense of love to love inspiring.   [60]

'Love makes earth the water drink,
Love to earth makes water sinke;
And if dumbe things be so witty,
Shall a heavenly grace want pitty? '

There his hands in their speech, faine   [65]
Would have made tongue's language plaine;
But her hands his hands repelling,
Gave repulse all grace excelling.

Then she spake; her speech was such,
As not eares but hart did tuch: [70]
While such wise she love denied,
As yet love she signified.

'*Astrophil*' sayd she, 'my love
Cease in these effects to prove:
Now be still, yet still beleeve me,   [75]
Thy griefe more then death would grieve me.

'If that any thought in me,
Can tast comfort but of thee,
Let me, fed with hellish anguish,
Joylesse, hopelesse, endlesse languish.   [80]

'If those eyes you praised, be
Half so deere as you to me,
Let me home returne, starke blinded
Of those eyes, and blinder minded.

'If to secret of my hart,   [85]
I do any wish impart,
Where thou art not formost placed,
Be both wish and I defaced.

'If more may be sayd, I say,
All my blisse in thee I lay;   [90]
If thou love, my love content thee,
For all love, all faith is meant thee.

'Trust me while I thee deny,
In my selfe the smart I try,

49

Tyran honour doth thus use thee,   [95]
Stella's selfe might not refuse thee.

'Therefore, Deere, this no more move,
Least, though I leave not thy love,
Which too deep in me is framed,
I should blush when thou art named.'   [100]

Therewithall away she went,
Leaving him so passion rent,
With what she had done and spoken,
That therewith my song is broken.

Ninth song

GO my flocke, go get you hence,
Seeke a better place of feeding,
Where you may have some defence
From the stormes in my breast breeding,
And showers from mine eyes proceeding.   [5]

Leave a wretch, in whom all wo
Can abide to keepe no measure,
Merry flocke, such one forgo,
Unto whom mirth is displeasure,
Only rich in mischiefe's treasure.   [10]

Yet alas before you go,
Heare your wofull maister's story,
Which to stones I els would show:
Sorrow onely then hath glory,
When tis excellently sory.   [15]

Stella fiercest shepherdesse,
Fiercest but yet fairest ever;
Stella whom ô heavens do blesse,
Tho against me shee persever,
Tho I blisse enherit never.   [20]

Stella hath refused me,
Stella who more love hath proved,
In this caitife hart to be,
Then can in good eawes be moved
Toward *Lamkins* best beloved.   [25]

Stella hath refused me,
Astrophil that so wel served,
In this pleasant spring must see
While in pride flowers be preserved,
Himselfe onely winter-sterved.   [30]

Why alas doth she then sweare,
That she loveth me so dearely,
Seing me so long to beare
Coles of love that burne so clearely,
And yet leave me helplesse meerely?   [35]

Is that love? forsooth I trow,
If I saw my good dog grieved,
And a helpe for him did know,
My love should not be beleeved,
But he were by me releeved.   [40]

No, she hates me, wellaway,
Faining love, somewhat to please me:
For she knowes, if she display
All her hate, death soone would seaze me,
And of hideous torments ease me.   [45]

Then adieu, deere flocke adieu:
But alas, if in your straying
Heavenly *Stella* meete with you,
Tell her in your piteous blaying,
Her poore slave's unjust decaying.   [50]

87   WHEN I was forst from *Stella* ever deere,
      Stella food of my thoughts, hart of my hart,
      Stella whose eyes make all my tempests cleere,
    By iron lawes of duty to depart:
        Alas I found, that she with me did smart,
    I saw that teares did in her eyes appeare;
    I saw that sighes her sweetest lips did part,
    And her sad words my sadded sence did heare.
        For me, I wept to see pearles scattered so,
      I sighd her sighes, and wailed for her wo,
    Yet swam in joy, such love in her was seene.
        Thus while th' effect most bitter was to me,
      And nothing then, the cause more sweet could be,
    I had bene vext, if vext I had not beene.

88   OUT traytour absence, darest thou counsell me,
    From my deare Captainnesse to run away?
    Because in brave array heere marcheth she,
    That to win me, oft shewes a present pay?
        Is faith so weake? Or is such force in thee?
    When Sun is hid, can starres such beames display?
    Cannot heavn's food, once felt, keepe stomakes free
    From base desire on earthly cates to pray?
        Tush absence, while thy mistes eclipse that light,
      My Orphan sence flies to the inward sight,
    Where memory sets foorth the beames of love.
        That where before hart loved and eyes did see,
      In hart both sight and love now coupled be;
    United powers make each the stronger prove.

89   NOW that of absence the most irksome night,
      With darkest shade doth overcome my day;
      Since *Stella's* eyes, wont to give me my day,
    Leaving my Hemisphere, leave me in night,
    Each day seemes long, and longs for long-staid night,
      The night as tedious, wooes th'approch of day;
      Tired with the dusty toiles of busie day,
    Languisht with horrors of the silent night,

Suffering the evils both of the day and night,
    While no night is more darke then is my day,
Nor no day hath lesse quiet then my night:
    With such bad mixture of my night and day,
That living thus in blackest winter night,
    I feele the flames of hottest sommer day.

STELLA thinke not that I by verse seeke fame,
    Who seeke, who hope, who love, who live but thee;
    Thine eyes my pride, thy lips my history:
If thou praise not, all other praise is shame.
Nor so ambitious am I, as to frame
    A nest for my yong praise in Lawrell tree:
    In truth I sweare, I wish not there should be
Graved in mine Epitaph a Poet's name:
    Ne if I would, could I just title make,
That any laud to me thereof should grow,
Without my plumes from others' wings I take.
For nothing from my wit or will doth flow,
    Since all my words thy beauty doth endite,
    And love doth hold my hand, and makes me write.

STELLA, while now by honour's cruell might,
    I am from you, light of my life, mis-led,
    And that faire you my Sunne, thus overspred
With absence' Vaile, I live in Sorowe's night.
If this darke place yet shew like candle light,
    Some beautie's peece, as amber colour'd hed,
    Milke hands, rose cheeks, or lips more sweet, more red,
Or seeing jets, blacke, but in blacknesse bright.
    They please I do confesse, they please mine eyes,
But why? because of you they models be,
Models such be wood-globes of glistring skies.
Deere, therefore be not jealous over me,
    If you heare that they seeme my hart to move,
    Not them, ô no, but you in them I love.

92   BE your words made (good Sir) of Indian ware,
      That you allow me them by so small rate?
      Or do you cutted Spartanes imitate?
Or do you meane my tender eares to spare,
That to my questions you so totall are?
      When I demaund of *Phenix Stella's* state,
      You say forsooth, you left her well of late.
O God, thinke you that satisfies my care?
      I would know whether she did sit or walke,
How cloth'd, how waited on, sighd she or smilde,
Whereof, with whom, how often did she talke,
With what pastime, time's journey she beguilde,
      If her lips daignd to sweeten my poore name.
      Say all, and all well sayd, still say the same.

Tenth song

O DEARE life, when shall it be,
      That mine eyes thine eyes may see?
      And in them thy mind discover,
      Whether absence have had force
      Thy remembrance to divorce,   [5]
      From the image of thy lover?

O if I my self find not;
      After parting ought forgot,
      Nor debard from beautie's treasure,
      Let no tongue aspire to tell,   [10]
      In what high joyes I shall dwell,
      Only thought aymes at the pleasure.

Thought therefore I will send thee,
      To take up the place for me;
      Long I will not after tary,   [15]
      There unseene thou maist be bold,
      Those faire wonders to behold,
      Which in them my hopes do cary.

Thought see thou no place forbeare,
    Enter bravely every where,   [20]
    Seaze on all to her belonging;
    But if thou wouldst garded be,
    Fearing her beames, take with thee
    Strength of liking, rage of longing.

Thinke of that most gratefull time,   [25]
    When my leaping hart will clime,
    In my lips to have his biding,
    There those roses for to kisse,
    Which do breath a sugred blisse,
    Opening rubies, pearles deviding.   [30]

Thinke of my most Princely power,
    When I blessed shall devower,
    With my greedy licorous sences,
    Beauty, musicke, sweetnesse, love
    While she doth against me prove   [35]
    Her strong darts, but weake defences.

Thinke, thinke of those dalyings,
    When with Dovelike murmurings,
    With glad moning passed anguish,
    We change eyes, and hart for hart,   [40]
    Each to other do imparte,
    Joying till joy make us languish.

O my thought my thoughts surcease,
    Thy delights my woes increase,
    My life melts with too much thinking;   [45]
    Thinke no more but die in me,
    Till thou shalt revived be,
    At her lips my Nectar drinking.

93   O FATE, ô fault, ô curse, child of my blisse,
        What sobs can give words grace my griefe to show?
        What inke is blacke inough to paint my wo?
    Through me, wretch me, even *Stella* vexed is.
    Yet truth (if Caitif's breath mighte call thee) this
        Witnesse with me, that my foule stumbling so,
        From carelesnesse did in no maner grow,
    But wit confus'd with too much care did misse.
        And do I then my selfe this vaine scuse give?
    I have (live I and know this) harmed thee,
    Tho worlds quite me, shall I my selfe forgive?
    Only with paines my paines thus eased be,
        That all thy hurts in my hart's wracke I reede;
        I cry thy sighs; my deere, thy teares I bleede.

94   GRIEFE find the words, for thou hast made my braine
        So darke with misty vapors, which arise
        From out thy heavy mould, that inbent eyes
    Can scarce discerne the shape of mine owne paine.
    Do thou then (for thou canst) do thou complaine,
        For my poore soule, which now that sicknesse tries,
        Which even to sence, sence of it selfe denies,
    Though harbengers of death lodge there his traine.
        Or if thy love of plaint yet mine forbeares,
    As of a caitife worthy so to die,
    Yet waile thy selfe, and waile with causefull teares,
    That though in wretchednesse thy life doth lie,
    Yet growest more wretched then thy nature beares,
    By being placed in such a wretch as I.

95   YET sighs, deere sighs, indeede true friends you are,
        That do not leave your least friend at the wurst,
        But as you with my breast I oft have nurst,
    So gratefull now you waite upon my care.
    Faint coward joy no longer tarry dare,
        Seeing hope yeeld when this wo strake him furst:
        Delight protests he is not for the accurst,
    Though oft himselfe my mate-in-armes he sware.

Nay sorrow comes with such maine rage, that he
Kils his owne children, teares, finding that they
By love were made apt to consort with me.
Only true sighs, you do not go away,
    Thanke may you have for such a thankfull part,
    Thanke-worthiest yet when you shall breake my hart.

6 THOUGHT with good cause thou likest so well the night,
    Since kind or chance gives both one liverie,
    Both sadly blacke, both blackly darkned be,
Night bard from Sun, thou from thy owne sunne's light;
Silence in both displaies his sullen might,
    Slow heavinesse in both holds one degree,
    That full of doubts, thou of perplexity;
Thy teares expresse night's native moisture right.
    In both a mazefull solitarinesse:
In night of sprites the gastly powers stur,
In thee or sprites or sprited gastlinesse:
    But, but (alas) night's side the ods hath fur,
    For that at length yet doth invite some rest,
    Thou though still tired, yet still doost it detest.

7 *DIAN* that faine would cheare her friend the Night,
    Shewes her oft at the full her fairest face,
    Bringing with her those starry Nimphs, whose chace
From heavenly standing hits each mortall wight.
But ah poore Night, in love with *Phœbus'* light,
    And endlesly dispairing of his grace,
    Her selfe (to shew no other joy hath place)
Silent and sad in mourning weedes doth dight:
    Even so (alas) a Lady *Dian's* peere,
With choise delights and rarest company,
Would faine drive cloudes from out my heavy cheere.
But wo is me, though joy it selfe were she,
    She could not shew my blind braine waies of joy,
    While I dispaire my Sunne's sight to enjoy.

98 A H bed, the field where joye's peace some do see,
   The field where all my thoughts to warre be traind,
   How is thy grace by my strange fortune staind!
  How thy lee shores by my sighes stormed be!
  With sweete soft shades thou oft invitest me
   To steale some rest, but wretch I am constraind,
   (Spurd with love's spur, though gald and shortly raind
  With care's hard hand) to turne and tosse in thee.
   While the blacke horrors of the silent night,
   Paint woe's blacke face so lively to my sight,
  That tedious leasure marks each wrinckled line:
   But when *Aurora* leades out *Phœbus'* daunce,
   Mine eyes then only winke, for spite perchance,
  That wormes should have their Sun, and I want mine.

99 W HEN far spent night perswades each mortall eye,
   To whom nor art nor nature graunteth light,
   To lay his then marke wanting shafts of sight,
  Clos'd with their quivers in sleep's armory;
  With windowes ope then most my mind doth lie,
   Viewing the shape of darknesse and delight,
   Takes in that sad hue, which with th'inward night
  Of his mazde powers keepes perfit harmony:
   But when birds charme, and that sweete aire, which is
  Morne's messenger, with rose enameld skies
  Cals each wight to salute the floure of blisse;
  In tombe of lids then buried are mine eyes,
   Forst by their Lord, who is asham'd to find
   Such light in sense, with such a darkned mind.

100 O TEARES, no teares, but raine from beautie's skies,
   Making those Lillies and those Roses grow,
   Which ay most faire, now more then most faire show,
  While gracefull pitty beauty beautifies.
  O honied sighs, which from that breast do rise,
   Whose pants do make unspilling creame to flow,
   Wing'd with whose breath, so pleasing *Zephires* blow,
  As can refresh the hell where my soule fries.

O plaints conserv'd in such a sugred phraise,
That eloquence it selfe envies your praise,
While sobd out words a perfect Musike give.
   Such teares, sighs, plaints, no sorrow is, but joy:
   Or if such heavenly signes must prove annoy,
All mirth farewell, let me in sorrow live.

STELLA is sicke, and in that sicke bed lies
Sweetnesse, that breathes and pants as oft as she:
And grace, sicke too, such fine conclusions tries,
That sickenesse brags it selfe best graced to be.
   Beauty is sicke, but sicke in so faire guise,
That in that palenesse beautie's white we see;
And joy, which is inseperate from those eyes,
Stella now learnes (strange case) to weepe in thee.
   Love moves thy paine, and like a faithfull page,
As thy lookes sturre, runs up and downe to make
All folkes prest at thy will thy paine to 'swage,
Nature with care sweates for her darling's sake,
   Knowing worlds passe, ere she enough can find
   Of such heaven stuffe, to cloath so heavenly mynde.

WHERE be those Roses gone, which sweetned so our eyes?
   Where those red cheeks, which oft with faire encrease did frame
   The height of honor in the kindly badge of shame?
Who hath the crimson weeds stolne from my morning skies?
How doth the colour vade of those vermillion dies,
   Which Nature' selfe did make, and selfe engraind the same?
   I would know by what right this palenesse overcame
That hue, whose force my hart still unto thraldome ties?
   Gallein's adoptive sonnes, who by a beaten way
   Their judgements hackney on, the fault on sicknesse lay,
But feeling proofe makes me say they mistake it furre:
   It is but love, which makes his paper perfit white
   To write therein more fresh the story of delight,
While beautie's reddest inke *Venus* for him doth sturre.

103   O HAPPIE Tems, that didst my *Stella* beare,
       I saw thy selfe with many a smiling line
       Upon thy cheerefull face, joye's livery weare:
       While those faire planets on thy streames did shine.
            The bote for joy could not to daunce forbeare,
       While wanton winds with beauties so devine
       Ravisht, staid not, till in her golden haire
       They did themselves (ô sweetest prison) twine.
            And faine those *Æols'* youthes there would their stay
       Have made, but forst by Nature still to flie,
       First did with puffing kisse those lockes display:
       She so discheveld, blusht; from window I
            With sight thereof cride out; ô faire disgrace,
            Let honor' selfe to thee graunt highest place.

104   ENVIOUS wits what hath bene mine offence,
            That with such poysonous care my lookes you marke,
            That to each word, nay sigh of mine you harke,
       As grudging me my sorrowe's eloquence?
       Ah, is it not enough, that I am thence,
            Thence, so farre thence, that scarcely any sparke
            Of comfort dare come to this dungeon darke,
       Where rigrows exile lockes up all my sense?
            But if I by a happy window passe,
       If I but stars upon mine armour beare,
       Sicke, thirsty, glad (though but of empty glasse:)
       Your morall notes straight my hid meaning teare
            From out my ribs, and puffing prove that I
            Do *Stella* love. Fooles, who doth it deny?

Eleventh song

       'WHO is it that this darke night,
       Underneath my window playneth?'
       It is one who from thy sight,
       Being (ah) exild, disdayneth
       Every other vulgar light.   [5]

'Why alas, and are you he?
Be not yet those fancies changed?'
Deere when you find change in me,
Though from me you be estranged,
Let my chaunge to ruine be.   [10]

'Well in absence this will dy,
Leave to see, and leave to wonder.'
Absence sure will helpe, if I
Can learne, how my selfe to sunder
From what in my hart doth ly.   [15]

'But time will these thoughts remove:
Time doth worke what no man knoweth.'
Time doth as the subject prove,
With time still th' affection groweth
In the faithfull Turtle dove.   [20]

'What if you new beauties see,
Will not they stir new affection?'
I will thinke theye pictures be,
(Image like of Saints' perfection)
Poorely counterfeting thee.   [25]

'But your reason's purest light,
Bids you leave such minds to nourish.'
Deere, do reason no such spite,
Never doth thy beauty florish
More then in my reason's sight.   [30]

'But the wrongs love beares, will make
Love at length leave undertaking.'
No, the more fooles it do shake,
In a ground of so firme making,
Deeper still they drive the stake.   [35]

'Peace, I thinke that some give eare:
Come no more, least I get anger.'
Blisse, I will my blisse forbeare,
Fearing (sweete) you to endanger,
But my soule shall harbour there.   [40]

61

'Well, be gone, be gone I say,
Lest that *Argus* eyes perceive you.'
O unjustest fortune's sway,
Which can make me thus to leave you,
And from lowts to run away.   [45]

105   UNHAPPIE sight, and hath she vanisht by
         So neere, in so good time, so free a place?
         Dead glasse, doost thou thy object so imbrace,
As what my hart still sees thou canst not spie?
I sweare by her I love and lacke, that I
         Was not in fault, who bent thy dazling race
         Onely unto the heav'n of *Stella's* face,
Counting but dust what in the way did lie.
         But cease mine eyes, your teares do witnesse well
That you, guiltlesse thereof, your Nectar mist:
Curst be the page from whome the bad torch fell,
Curst be the night which did your strife resist,
         Curst be the Cochman which did drive so fast,
         With no worse curse then absence makes me tast.

106   O ABSENT presence *Stella* is not here;
         False flattering hope, that with so faire a face,
         Bare me in hand, that in this Orphane place,
Stella, I say my *Stella*, should appeare.
What saist thou now, where is that dainty cheere
         Thou toldst mine eyes should helpe their famisht case?
         But thou art gone, now that selfe felt disgrace
Doth make me most to wish thy comfort neere.
         But heere I do store of faire Ladies meete,
         Who may with charme of conversation sweete,
Make in my heavy mould new thoughts to grow:
         Sure they prevaile as much with me, as he
         That bad his friend, but then new maim'd, to be
Mery with him, and not thinke of his woe.

STELLA since thou so right a Princesse art
    Of all the powers which life bestowes on me,
    That ere by them ought undertaken be,
They first resort unto that soueraigne part;
Sweete, for a while give respite to my hart,
    Which pants as though it still should leape to thee:
    And on my thoughts give thy Lieftenancy
To this great cause, which needs both use and art,
    And as a Queene, who from her presence sends
Whom she imploies, dismisse from thee my wit,
Till it have wrought what thy owne will attends.
On servants' shame oft Maister's blame doth sit;
    O let not fooles in me thy workes reprove,
    And scorning say, 'See what it is to love.'

WHEN sorrow (using mine owne fier's might)
    Melts downe his lead into my boyling brest,
    Through that darke fornace to my hart opprest,
There shines a joy from thee my only light;
But soone as thought of thee breeds my delight,
    And my yong soule flutters to thee his nest,
    Most rude dispaire my daily unbidden guest,
Clips streight my wings, streight wraps me in his night,
    And makes me then bow downe my head, and say,
Ah what doth *Phœbus'* gold that wretch availe,
Whom iron doores do keepe from use of day?
So strangely (alas) thy works in me prevaile,
    That in my woes for thee thou art my joy,
    And in my joyes for thee my only annoy.

Delia.

Contayning certayne
Sonnets: vvith the
complaint of
Rosamond.
(.·.)

 Aetas prima canat Veneres
postrema tumultus.

AT LONDON,
Printed by I. C. for Si-
mon Waterson, dwelling in
Paules Church-yard at
the signe of the Crowne.
1592.

TO THE RIGHT HO-
nourable the Ladie *Mary*,
Countesse of Pembroke.

Right honorable, although I rather desired to keep in the priuate passions of my youth, from the multitude, as things vtterd to my selfe, and consecrated to silence: yet seeing I was betraide by the indiscretion of a greedie Printer, and had some of my secrets bewraide to the world, vncorrected: doubting the like of the rest, I am forced to publish that which I neuer ment. But this wrong was not onely doone to mee, but to him whose vnmatchable lines haue indured the like misfortune; Ignorance sparing not to commit sacriledge vpon so holy Reliques. Yet Astrophel, flying with the wings of his own fame, a higher pitch then the gross-sighted can discerne, hath registred his owne name in the Annals of eternitie, and cannot be disgraced, howsoeuer disguised. And for my selfe, seeing I am thrust out into the worlde, and that my vnboldned Muse, is forced to appeare so rawly in publique; I desire onely to bee graced by the countenance of your protection: whome the fortune of our time hath made the happie and iudiciall Patronesse of the Muses, (a glory hereditary to your house) to preserue them from those hidious Beastes, Obliuion, and Barbarisme. Whereby you doe not onely possesse the honour of the present, but also do bind posterity to an euer gratefull memorie of your vertues, wherein you must suruiue your selfe. And if my lines heereafter better laboured, shall purchase grace in the world, they must remaine the monuments of your honourable fauour, and recorde the zealous duetie of mee, who am vowed to your honour in all obseruancy for euer,

Samuel Danyell.

(9)

TO DELIA.

Vnto the boundles Ocean of thy beautie
Runs this poore riuer, charg'd with streames of zeale:
Returning thee the tribute of my dutie,
Which heere my loue, my youth, my playnts reueale.
Heere I vnclaspe the booke of my charg'd soule,
Where I haue cast th'accounts of all my care:
Heere haue I summ'd my sighes, heere I enroule
Howe they were spent for thee; Looke what they are.
Looke on the deere expences of my youth,
And see how iust I reckon with thyne eyes,
Examine well thy beautie with my trueth,
And crosse my cares ere greater summes arise.
Reade it sweet maide, though it be doone but slightly;
Who can shewe all his loue, doth loue but lightly.

Sonnet

Goe wailing verse, the infants of my loue,
Minerua-like, brought foorth without a Mother:
Present the image of the cares I proue,
Witnes your Fathers griefe exceedes all other.
Sigh out a story of her cruell deedes,
With interrupted accents of dispayre:
A Monument that whosoeuer reedes,
May iustly praise, and blame my loueles Faire.
Say her disdaine hath dryed vp my blood,
And starued you, in succours still denying:
Presse to her eyes, importune me some good;
Waken her sleeping pittie with your crying.
Knock at that hard hart, beg till you haue moou'd her;
And tell th'vnkind, how deerely I haue lou'd her.

Sonnet
II.

Sonnet
III.

If so it hap this of-spring of my care,
These fatall Antheames, sad and mornefull Songes:
Come to their view, who like afflicted are;
Let them yet sigh their owne, and mone my wrongs.

    But vntouch'd harts, with vnaffected eye,
Approch not to behold so great distresse:
Cleer-sighted you, soone note what is awry,
Whilst blinded ones mine errours neuer gesse.

    You blinded soules whom youth and errours lead,
You outcast Eglets, dazled with your sunne:
Ah you, and none but you my sorrowes read,
You best can iudge the wrongs that she hath dunne.

        That she hath doone, the motiue of my paine;
        Who whilst I loue, doth kill me with disdaine.

Sonnet
IIII.

    These plaintiue verse, the Posts of my desire,
Which haste for succour to her slowe regarde:
Beare not report of any slender fire,
Forging a griefe to winne a fames rewarde.

    Nor are my passions limnd for autward hewe,
For that no collours can depaynt my sorrowes:
Delia her selfe, and all the world may viewe
Best in my face, how cares hath til'd deepe forrowes.

    No Bayes I seeke to deck my mourning brow,
O cleer-eyde Rector of the holie Hill:
My humble accents craue the Olyue bow,
Of her milde pittie and relenting will.

        These lines I vse, t'vnburthen mine owne hart;
        My loue affects no fame, nor steemes of art.

Sonnet
V.

    Whilst youth and error led my wandring minde,
And set my thoughts in heedeles waies to range:
All vnawares a Goddesse chaste I finde,
Diana-like, to worke my suddaine change.

    For her no sooner had my view bewrayd,
But with disdaine to see me in that place:
With fairest hand, the sweet vnkindest maide,
Castes water-bold disdaine vpon my face.

68

Which turn'd my sport into a Harts dispaire,
Which still is chac'd, whilst I haue any breath,
By mine owne thoughts: set on me by my faire,
My thoughts like houndes, pursue me to my death.
    Those that I fostred of mine owne accord,
    Are made by her to murther thus their Lord.

Faire is my loue, and cruell as sh'is faire;   Sonnet
Her brow shades frownes, although her eyes are sunny;   VI.
Her Smiles are lightning, though her pride dispaire;
And her disdaines are gall; her fauours hunny.
    A modest maide, deckt with a blush of honour,
Whose feete doe treade greene pathes of youth and loue,
The wonder of all eyes that looke vppon her:
Sacred on earth, design'd a Saint aboue.
    Chastitie and Beautie, which were deadly foes,
Liue reconciled friends within her brow:
And had she pittie to conioine with those,
Then who had heard the plaints I vtter now.
    O had she not beene faire, and thus vnkinde,
    My Muse had slept, and none had knowne my minde.

O had she not beene faire and thus vnkinde,   Sonnet
Then had no finger pointed at my lightnes: VII.
The world had neuer knowne what I doe finde,
And Clowdes obscure had shaded still her brightnes.
    Then had no Censors eye these lines suruaide,
Nor grauer browes haue iudg'd my Muse so vaine;
No sunne my blush and errour had bewraide,
Nor yet the world had heard of such disdaine.
    Then had I walkt with bold erected face,
No down-cast looke had signified my mis:
But my degraded hopes, with such disgrace
Did force me grone out griefes, and vtter this.
    For being full, should not I then haue spoken:
    My sence oppres'd, had fail'd; and hart had broken.

Sonnet
VIII.

Thou poore hart sacrifiz'd vnto the fairest,
Hast sent the incens of thy sighes to heauen:
And still against her frownes fresh vowes repayrest,
And made thy passions with her beautie euen.

And you mine eyes the agents of my hart,
Told the dumbe message of my hidden griefe:
And oft with carefull turnes, with silent art,
Did treate the cruell Fayre to yeelde reliefe.

And you my verse, the Aduocates of loue,
Haue followed hard the processe of my case:
And vrg'd that title which dooth plainely proue,
My faith should win, if iustice might haue place.

Yet though I see, that nought we doe can moue her,
Tis not disdaine must make me leaue to loue her.

Sonnet
IX.

If this be loue, to drawe a weary breath,
Painte on flowdes, till the shore, crye to th'ayre:
With downward lookes, still reading on the earth,
The sad memorials of my loues despaire.

If this be loue, to warre against my soule,
Lye downe to waile, rise vp to sigh and grieue me:
The neuer-resting stone of care to roule,
Still to complaine my greifes, and none releiue me.

If this be loue, to cloath me with darke thoughts,
Haunting vntroden pathes to waile apart;
My pleasures horror, Musique tragicke notes,
Teares in my eyes, and sorrowe at my hart.

If this be loue, to liue a liuing death;
O then loue I, and drawe this weary breath.

Sonnet
X.

O then I loue, and drawe this weary breath,
For her the cruell faire, within whose brow
I written finde the sentence of my death,
In vnkinde letters; wrought she cares not how.

O thou that rul'st the confines of the night,
Laughter-louing Goddesse, worldly pleasures Queene,
Intenerat that hart that sets so light,
The truest loue that euer yet was seene.

And cause her leaue to triumph in this wise,
Vppon the prostrate spoyle of that poore harte:
That serues a trophey to her conquering eyes,
And must their glorie to the world imparte.

      Once let her know, sh'hath done enough to proue me;
      And let her pittie if she cannot loue me.

Teares, vowes, and prayers win the hardest hart:
Teares, vowes, and prayers haue I spent in vaine;
Teares, cannot soften flint, nor vowes conuart,
Prayers preuaile not with a quaint disdaine.

    I lose my teares, where I haue lost my loue,
I vowe my faith, where faith is not regarded;
I pray in vaine, a merciles to moue:
So rare a faith ought better be rewarded.

    Yet though I cannot win her will with teares,
Though my soules Idoll scorneth all my vowes;
Though all my prayers be to so deafe eares:
No fauour though the cruell faire allowes.

      Yet will I weepe, vowe, pray to cruell Shee:
      Flint, Frost, Disdaine, weares, melts, and yeelds we see.

Sonnet
XI.

My spotles loue hoouers with white wings,
About the temple of the proudest frame:
Where blaze those lights fayrest of earthly things,
Which cleere our clouded world with brightest flame.

    M'ambitious thoughts confined in her face,
Affect no honour, but what she can giue mee:
My hopes doe rest in limits of her grace,
I weygh no comfort vnlesse she releeue mee.

    For she that can my hart imparadize,
Holdes in her fairest hand what deerest is:
My fortunes wheele, the circle of her eyes,
Whose rowling grace deigne once a turne of blis.

      All my liues sweete consists in her alone,
      So much I loue the most vnlouing one.

Sonnet
XII.

71

Sonnet
XIII.

Behold what happe *Pigmaleon* had to frame,
And carue his proper griefe vpon a stone:
My heauie fortune is much like the same,
I worke on Flint, and that's the cause I mone.

 For haples loe euen with mine owne desires,
I figured on the table of my harte,
The fayrest forme, the worldes eye admires,
And so did perish by my proper arte.

 And still I toile, to chaunge the marble brest
Of her, whose sweetest grace I doe adore:
Yet cannot finde her breathe vnto my rest,
Hard is her hart and woe is me therefore.

  O happie he that ioy'd his stone and arte,
  Vnhappy ! to loue a stony harte.

Sonnet
XIIII.

Those amber locks, are those same nets my deere,
Wherewith my libertie thou didst surprize:
Loue was the flame, that fired me so neere,
The darte transpearsing, were those Christall eyes.

 Strong is the net, and feruent is the flame;
Deepe is the wounde, my sighes do well report:
Yet doe I loue, adore, and praise the same,
That holdes, that burnes, that wounds me in this sort.

 And list not seeke to breake, to quench, to heale,
The bonde, the flame, the wound that festreth so;
By knife, by lyquor, or by salue to deale.
So much I please to perish in my wo.

  Yet least long trauailes be aboue my strength,
  Good *Delia* lose, quench, heale me now at length.

Sonnet
XV.

If that a loyall hart and faith vnfained,
If a sweete languish with a chast desire:
If hunger-staruen thoughts so long retayned,
Fed but with smoake, and cherisht but with fire.

 And if a brow with cares caracters painted,
Bewraies my loue, with broken words halfe spoken,
To her that sits in my thoughts Temple sainted,
And layes to view my Vultur-gnawne hart open.

72

If I haue doone due homage to her eyes,
And had my sighes styll tending on her name:
If on her loue my life and honour lyes;
And she th'vnkindest maide still scornes the same.
　　Let this suffice, the world yet may see;
　　The fault is hers, though mine the hurt must bee.

Happie in sleepe, waking content to languish,
Imbracing cloudes by night, in day time morne:
All things I loath saue her and mine owne anguish,
Pleas'd in my hurt, inur'd to liue forlorne.
　　Nought doe I craue, but loue, death, or my Lady,
Hoarce with crying mercy, mercy yet my merit;
So many vowes and prayers euer made I,
That now at length t'yeelde, meere pittie were it.
　　But still the *Hydra* of my cares renuing,
Reuiues new sorrowes of her fresh disdayning;
Still must I goe the Summer windes pursuing:
Finding no ende nor Period of my payning.
　　Waile all my life, my griefes do touch so neerely,
　　And thus I liue, because I loue her deerely.

Since the first looke that led me to this error,
To this thoughts-maze, to my confusion tending:
Still haue I liu'd in griefe, in hope, in terror,
The circle of my sorrowes neuer ending.
　　Yet cannot leaue her loue that holdes me hatefull,
Her eyes exact it, though her hart disdaines mee:
See what reward he hath that serues th'vngratefull,
So true and loyall loue no fauours gaines mee.
　　Still must I whet my younge desires abated,
Vppon the Flint of such a hart rebelling;
And all in vaine, her pride is so innated,
She yeeldes no place at all for pitties dwelling.
　　Oft haue I tolde her that my soule did loue her,
　　And that with teares, yet all this will not moue her.

Sonnet
XVIII.

Restore thy tresses to the golden Ore,
Yeelde *Cithereas* sonne those Arkes of loue;
Bequeath the heauens the starres that I adore,
And to th'Orient do thy Pearles remoue.

Yeelde thy hands pride vnto th'yuory whight,
T'*Arabian* odors giue thy breathing sweete:
Restore thy blush vnto *Aurora* bright,
To *Thetis* giue the honour of thy feete.

Let *Venus* haue thy graces, her resign'd,
And thy sweete voyce giue backe vnto the Spheares:
But yet restore thy fearce and cruell minde,
To *Hyrcan* Tygers, and to ruthles Beares.

Yeelde to the Marble thy hard hart againe;
So shalt thou cease to plague, and I to paine.

Sonnet
XIX.

If Beautie thus be clouded with a frowne,
That pittie shines no comfort to my blis:
And vapors of disdaine so ouergrowne,
That my liues light thus wholy darkned is.

Why should I more molest the world with cryes?
The ayre with sighes, the earth belowe with teares?
Since I liue hatefull to those ruthlesse eyes,
Vexing with vntun'd moane, her daintie eares.

If I haue lou'd her deerer then my breath,
My breath that calls the heauens to witnes it:
And still must holde her deere till after death.
And if that all this cannot moue a whit;

Yet let her say that she hath doone me wrong,
To vse me thus and knowe I lou'd so long.

Sonnet
XX.

Come death the Anchor-holde of all my thoughtes,
My last Resort whereto my soule appealeth;
For all too long on earth my fancy dotes,
Whilst my best blood my younge desiers sealeth.

That hart is now the prospectiue of horror,
That honored hath the cruelst faire that lyueth:
The cruelst faire, that sees I languish for her,
Yet neuer mercy to my merit giueth.

This is her Lawrell and her triumphes prize,
To tread me downe with foote of her disgrace:
Whilst I did builde my fortune in her eyes,
And laide my liues rest on so faire a face;
    That rest I lost, my loue, my life and all,
    So high attempts to lowe disgraces fall.

These sorrowing sighes, the smoakes of mine annoy;
These teares, which heate of sacred flame distils;

Are these due tributes that my faith dooth pay
Vnto the tyrant; whose vnkindnes kils.
  I sacrifize my youth, and blooming yeares,
At her proud feete, and she respects not it:
My flowre vntimely's withred with my teares,
And winter woes, for spring of youth vnfit.
  She thinkes a looke may recompence my care,
And so with lookes prolongs my long-lookt ease:
As short that blisse, so is the comfort rare,
Yet must that blisse my hungry thoughts appease.
    Thus she returnes my hopes so fruitlesse euer,
    Once let her loue indeede, or eye me neuer.

False hope prolongs my euer certaine griefe;
Traytrous to me and faithfull to my loue:
A thousand times it promis'd me reliefe,
Yet neuer any true effect I proue.
  Oft when I finde in her no trueth at all,
I banish her, and blame her trechery:
Yet soone againe I must her backe recall,
As one that dyes without her company.
  Thus often as I chase my hope from mee,
Straight way she hastes her vnto *Delias* eyes:
Fed with some pleasing looke there shall she bee,
And so sent backe and thus my fortune lyes.
    Lookes feede my Hope, Hope fosters me in vaine;
    Hopes are vnsure, when certaine is my paine.

Sonnet XXI.

Sonnet XXII.

Sonnet
XXIII.

Cloud

Looke in my griefes, and blame me not to morne,
From care to care that leades a life so bad;
Th'Orphan of fortune, borne to be her scorne,
Whose clouded brow dooth make my daies so sad.

Long are their nights whose cares doe neuer sleepe
Loathsome their daies, whome no sunne euer ioyde:
Her fairest eyes doe penetrate so deepe,
That thus I liue booth day and night annoyde.

But since the sweetest roote doth yeeld thus much,
Her praise from my complaint I may not part:
I loue th'effect for that the cause is such,
Ile praise her face, and blame her flintie hart.

    Whilst that wee make the world admire at vs,
    Her for disdaine, and me for louing thus.

Sonnet
XXIIII.

Oft and in vaine my rebel thoughts haue ventred,
To stop the passage of my vanquisht hart:
And shut those waies my friendly foe first entred,
Hoping thereby to free my better part.

And whilst I garde these windowes of this forte,
Where my harts theefe to vexe me made her choice:
And thether all my forces doe transporte,
An other passage opens at her voice.

Her voyce betraies me to her hand and eye:
My freedomes tyrants conquering all by arte:
But ah, what glorie can she get thereby,
With three such powers to plague one silly harte.

    Yet my soules soueraigne, since I must resigne;
    Reigne in my thoughts, my loue and life are thine.

Sonnet
XXV.

Raigne in my thoughts faire hand, sweete eye, rare voyce,
Possesse me whole, my harts triumuirat:
Yet heauie hart to make so hard a choise,
Of such as spoile thy poore afflicted state,

For whilst they striue which shall be Lord of all,
All my poore life by them is troden downe:
They all erect their Trophies on my fall,
And yeelde me nought that giues them their renowne.

When backe I looke, I sigh my freedome past,
And waile the state wherein I present stande:
And see my fortune euer like to last,
Finding me rain'd with such a heauie hande;
> What can I doo but yeeld, and yeeld I doo,
> And serue all three, and yet they spoile me too.

Whilst by her eyes pursu'd, my poore hart flew it,
Into the sacred bosome of my deerest:
She there in that sweete sanctuary slew it,
Where it presum'd his safetie to be neerest.
My priuiledge of faith could not protect it,
That was with blood and three yeeres witnes signed:
In all which time she neuer could suspect it,
For well she sawe my loue, and how I pined.
And yet no comfort would her brow reueale mee,
No lightning looke, which falling hopes erecteth:
What bootes to lawes of succour to appeale mee?
Ladies and tyrants, neuer lawes respecteth.
> Then there I dye, where hop'd I to haue liuen;
> And by that hand, which better might haue giuen.

Sonnet
XXVI.

The starre of my mishappe impos'd this payning,
To spend the Aprill of my yeers in wayling,
That neuer found my fortune but in wayning,
With still fresh cares my present woes assayling.
Yet her I blame not, though she might haue blest mee,
But my desires wings so high aspiring:
Now melted with the sunne that hath possest mee,
Downe doe I fall from off my high desiring;
And in my fall doe cry for mercy speedy,
No pittying eye lookes backe vppon my mourning:
No helpe I finde when now most fauour neede I,
Th'Ocean of my teares must drowne me burning,
> And this my death shall christen her anew,
> And giue the cruell Faire her tytle dew.

Sonnet
XXVII.

77

Sonnet
XXVIII.

     Raysing my hopes on hills of high desire,
Thinking to skale the heauen of her hart:
My slender meanes presum'd too high a part;
Her thunder of disdaine forst me retire;
     And threw mee downe to paine in all this fire,
Where loe I languish in so heauie smart,
Because th'attempt was farre aboue my arte:
Her pride brook'd not poore soules shold come so nye her.
     Yet I protest my high aspyring will,
Was not to dispossesse her of her right:
Her soueraignty should haue remayned still,
I onely sought the blisse to haue her sight.
       Her sight contented thus to see me spill,
       Fram'd my desires fit for her eyes to kill.

Sonnet
XXIX.

     O why dooth *Delia* credite so her glasse,
Gazing her beautie deign'd her by the skyes:
And dooth not rather looke on him (alas)
Whose state best shewes the force of murthering eyes.
     The broken toppes of loftie trees declare,
The fury of a mercy-wanting storme:
And of what force your wounding graces are,
Vppon my selfe you best may finde the forme.
     Then leaue your glasse, and gaze your selfe on mee,
That Mirrour shewes what powre is in your face:
To viewe your forme too much, may daunger bee,
Narcissus chaung'd t'a flowre in such a case.
       And you are chaung'd, but not t'a Hiacint;
       I feare your eye hath turn'd your hart to flint.

Sonnet
XXX.

     I once may see when yeeres shall wrecke my wronge,
When golden haires shall chaunge to siluer wyer:
And those bright rayes, that kindle all this fyer
Shall faile in force, their working not so stronge.
     Then beautie, now the burthen of my song,
Whose glorious blaze the world dooth so admire;
Must yeelde vp all to tyrant Times desire:
Then fade those flowres which deckt her pride so long.

When if she grieue to gaze her in her glas,
Which then presents her winter-withered hew;
Goe you my verse, goe tell her what she was;
For what she was she best shall finde in you.
    Your firie heate lets not her glorie passe,
    But Phenix-like shall make her liue anew.

Looke *Delia* how wee steeme the half-blowne Rose, Sonnet XXXI.
The image of thy blush and Summers honor:
Whilst in her tender greene she doth inclose
That pure sweete beautie, Time bestowes vppon her.
  No sooner spreades her glorie in the ayre,
But straight her ful-blowne pride is in declyning;
She then is scorn'd that late adorn'd the fayre:
So clowdes thy beautie, after fayrest shining.
  No Aprill can reuiue thy withred flowers,
Whose blooming grace adornes thy glorie now:
Swift speedy Time, feathred with flying howers,
Dissolues the beautie of the fairest brow.
    O let not then such riches waste in vaine;
    But loue whilst that thou maist be lou'd againe.

But loue whilst that thou maist be lou'd againe, Sonnet XXXII.
Now whilst thy May hath fill'd thy lappe with flowers;
Now whilst thy beautie beares without a staine;
Now vse thy Summer smiles ere winter lowres.
  And whilst thou spread'st vnto the rysing sunne,
The fairest flowre that euer sawe the light:
Now ioye thy time before thy sweete be dunne,
And *Delia,* thinke thy morning must haue night.
  And that thy brightnes sets at length to west:
When thou wilt close vp that which now thou showest:
And thinke the same becomes thy fading best,
Which then shall hide it most, and couer lowest.
    Men doe not weigh the stalke for that it was,
    When once they finde her flowre, her glory passe.

Sonnet
XXXIII.

When men shall finde thy flowre, thy glory passe,
And thou with carefull brow sitting alone:
Receiued hast this message from thy glasse,
That tells thee trueth, and saies that all is gone.

Fresh shalt thou see in mee the woundes thou madest,
Though spent thy flame, in mee the heate remayning:
I that haue lou'd thee thus before thou fadest,
My faith shall waxe, when thou art in thy wayning.

The world shall finde this miracle in mee,
That fire can burne, when all the matter's spent:
Then what my faith hath beene thy selfe shalt see,
And that thou wast vnkinde thou maiest repent.

Thou maist repent, that thou hast scorn'd my teares,
When Winter snowes vppon thy golden heares.

Sonnet
XXXIIII.

When Winter snowes vpon thy golden heares,
And frost of age hath nipt thy flowers neere:
When darke shall seeme thy day that neuer cleares,
And all lyes withred that was held so deere.

Then take this picture which I heere present thee,
Limned with a Pensill not all vnworthy:
Heere see the giftes that God and nature lent thee;
Heere read thy selfe, and what I suffred for thee.

This may remaine thy lasting monument,
Which happily posteritie may cherish:
These collours with thy fading are not spent;
These may remaine, when thou and I shall perish.

If they remaine, then thou shalt liue thereby;
They will remaine, and so thou canst not dye.

Sonnet
XXXV.

Thou canst not dye whilst any zeale abounde
In feeling harts, that can conceiue these lines:
Though thou a *Laura* hast no *Petrarch* founde,
In base attire, yet cleerely Beautie shines.

And I, though borne in a colder clime,
Doe feele mine inward heate as great, I knowe it:
He neuer had more faith, although more rime,
I loue as well, though he could better shew it.

But I may ad one feather to thy fame,
To helpe her flight throughout the fairest Ile:
And if my penne could more enlarge thy name,
Then shouldst thou liue in an immortall stile.
     But though that *Laura* better limned bee,
     Suffice, thou shalt be lou'd as well as shee.

O be not grieu'd that these my papers should,
Bewray vnto the world howe faire thou art:
Or that my wits haue shew'd the best they could,
The chastest flame that euer warmed hart.
   Thinke not sweete *Delia,* this shall be thy shame,
My Muse should sound thy praise with mournefull warble:
How many liue, the glory of whose name,
Shall rest in yce, when thine is grau'd in Marble.
   Thou maist in after ages liue esteem'd,
Vnburied in these lines reseru'd in purenes;
These shall intombe those eyes, that haue redeem'd
Mee from the vulgar, thee from all obscurenes.
     Although my carefull accents neuer mou'd thee;
     Yet count it no disgrace that I haue lou'd thee.

Delia these eyes that so admireth thine,
Haue seene those walles the which ambition reared,
To checke the world, how they intombd haue lyen
Within themselues; and on them ploughes haue eared.
   Yet for all that no barbarous hand attaynde,
The spoyle of fame deseru'd by vertuous men:
Whose glorious actions luckely had gainde,
Th'eternall Annals of a happie pen.
   Why then though *Delia* fade let that not moue her,
Though time do spoyle her of the fairest vaile
That euer yet mortallitie did couer;
Which shall instarre the needle and the trayle.
     That grace, that vertue, all that seru'd t'in-woman;
     Dooth her vnto eternitie assommon.

Sonnet XXXVIII.

Faire and louely maide, looke from the shore,
See thy *Leander* striuing in these waues:
Poore soule fore-spent, whose force can doe no more,
Now send foorth hopes, for now calme pittie saues.

And wafte him to thee with those louely eyes,
A happy conuoy to a holy lande:
Now shew thy powre, and where thy vertue lyes,
To saue thine owne, stretch out the fayrest hand.

Stretch out the fairest hand a pledge of peace,
That hand that dartes so right, and neuer misses:
Ile not reuenge olde wrongs, my wrath shall cease;
For that which gaue me woundes, Ile giue it kisses.

Once let the Ocean of my cares finde shore,
That thou be pleas'd, and I may sigh no more.

Sonnet XXXIX.

Reade in my face, a volume of despayres,
The wayling Hiades of my tragicke wo;
Drawne with my bloud, and printed with my cares,
Wrought by her hand, that I haue honoured so.

Who whilst I burne, she singes at my soules wrack,
Looking a loft from Turret of her pride:
There my soules tyrant ioyes her, in the sack
Of her owne seate, whereof I made her guide.

There doe these smoakes that from affliction ryse,
Serue as an incense to a cruell Dame:
A Sacrifize thrice gratefull to her eyes,
Because their powre serue to exact the same.

Thus ruines she, to satisfie her will;
The Temple, where her name was honored still.

Sonnet XL.

My *Cynthia* hath the waters of mine eyes,
The ready handmaides on her grace attending:
That neuer fall to ebbe, nor euer dryes,
For to their flowe she neuer graunts an ending.

Th'Ocean neuer did attende more duely,
Vppon his Soueraignes course, the nights pale Queene:
Nor paide the impost of his waues more truely,
Then mine to her in truth haue euer beene.

Yet nought the rocke of that hard hart can moue,
Where beate these teares with zeale, and fury driueth:
And yet I rather languish in her loue
Then I would ioy the fayrest she that liueth.
    I doubt to finde such pleasure in my gayning,
    As now I taste in compas of complayning.

How long shall I in mine affliction morne,   Sonnet
A burthen to my selfe, distress'd in minde: XLI.
When shall my interdicted hopes returne,
From out despayre wherein they liue confin'd.
    When shall her troubled browe charg'd with disdaine,
Reueale the treasure which her smyles impart:
When shall my faith the happinesse attaine,
To breake the yce that hath congeald her hart.
    Vnto her selfe, her selfe my loue dooth sommon,
If loue in her hath any powre to moue:
And let her tell me as she is a woman,
Whether my faith hath not deseru'd her loue.
        I knowe she cannot but must needes confesse it,
        Yet deignes not with one simple signe t'expresse it.

Beautie, sweet loue, is like the morning dewe,   Sonnet
Whose short refresh vpon the tender greene,   XLII.
Cheeres for a time but tyll the Sunne doth shew,
And straight tis gone as it had neuer beene.
    Soone doth it fade that makes the fairest florish,
Short is the glory of the blushing Rose,
The hew which thou so carefully doost nourish,
Yet which at length thou must be forc'd to lose.
    When thou surcharg'd with burthen of thy yeeres,
Shalt bend thy wrinkles homeward to the earth:
When tyme hath made a pasport for thy feares,
Dated in age the Kalends of our death.
        But ah no more, thys hath beene often tolde,
        And women grieue to thinke they must be old.

83

I must not grieue my Loue, whose eyes would reede,
Lines of delight, whereon her youth might smyle:
Flowers haue a tyme before they come to seede,
And she is young and now must sport the while.

Ah sport sweet Mayde in season of these yeeres,
And learne to gather flowers before they wither:
And where the sweetest blossoms first appeares,
Let loue and youth conduct thy pleasures thither.

Lighten forth smyles to cleere the clowded ayre,
And calme the tempest which my sighes doe rayse:
Pittie and smyles doe best become the fayre,
Pittie and smyles shall yeeld thee lasting prayse.

I hope to say when all my griefes are gone,
Happy the hart that sigh'd for such a one.

Drawne with th'attractiue vertue of her eyes,
My toucht hart turnes it to that happie cost:
My ioyfull North, where all my fortune lyes,
The leuell of my hopes desired most.

There where my *Delia* fayrer then the sunne,
Deckt with her youth whereon the world smyleth:
Ioyes in that honour which her beautic wonne,
Th'eternall volume which her fame compyleth.

Florish faire *Albion,* glory of the North,
Neptunes darling helde betweene his armes:
Deuided from the world as better worth,
Kept for himselfe, defended from all harmes.

Still let disarmed peace decke her and thee;
And Muse-foe *Mars,* abroade farre fostred bee.

Care-charmer sleepe, sonne of the Sable night,
Brother to death, in silent darknes borne:
Relieue my languish, and restore the light,
With darke forgetting of my cares returne.

And let the day be time enough to morne,
The shipwrack of my ill-aduentred youth;
Let waking eyes suffice to wayle theyr scorne,
Without the torment of the nights vntruth.

Cease dreames, th'ymagery of our day desires,
To modell foorth the passions of the morrow:
Neuer let rysing Sunne approue you lyers,
To adde more griefe to aggrauat my sorrow.
　　Still let me sleepe, imbracing clowdes in vaine;
　　And neuer wake, to feele the dayes disdayne.

Let others sing of Knights and Palladines,
In aged accents, and vntimely words:
Paint shadowes in imaginary lines,
Which well the reach of their high wits records;
But I must sing of thee and those faire eyes,
Autentique shall my verse in time to come,
When yet th'vnborne shall say, loe where she lyes,
Whose beautie made him speake that els was dombe
　These are the Arkes the Tropheis I erect,
That fortifie thy name against old age,
And these thy sacred vertues must protect,
Against the Darke and times consuming rage.
　　Though th'error of my youth they shall discouer,
　　Suffice they shew I liu'd and was thy louer.

Like as the Lute that ioyes or els dislikes,
As is his arte that playes vpon the same:
So sounds my Muse according as she strikes,
On my hart strings high tun'd vnto her fame.
　Her touch doth cause the warble of the sound,
Which heere I yeeld in lamentable wise,
A wailing deskant on the sweetest ground,
Whose due reports giue honor to her eyes.
　Els harsh my style, vntunable my Muse,
Hoarce sounds the voyce that prayseth not her name:
If any pleasing realish heere I vse,
Then iudge the world her beautie giues the same.
　　O happie ground that makes the musique such,
　　And blessed hand that giues so sweete a tuch.

Sonnet
XLVIII.

None other fame myne vnambitious Muse,
Affected euer but t'eternize thee:
All other honours doe my hopes refuse,
Which meaner priz'd and momentarie bee.

For God forbid I should my papers blot,
With mercynary lines, with seruile pen:
Praising vertues in them that haue them not,
Basely attending on the hopes of men.

No no my verse respects nor Thames nor Theaters,
Nor seekes it to be knowne vnto the Great:
But *Auon* rich in fame, though poore in waters,
Shall haue my song, where *Delia* hath her seate.

    Auon shall be my Thames, and she my Song;
    Ile sound her name the Ryuer all along.

Sonnet
XLIX.

Vnhappy pen and ill accepted papers,
That intimate in vaine my chaste desiers,
My chaste desiers, the euer burning tapers,
Inkindled by her eyes celestiall fiers.

Celestiall fiers and vnrespecting powers,
That deigne not view the glory of your might,
In humble lines the worke of carefull howers,
The sacrifice I offer to her sight.

But sith she scornes her owne, this rests for me,
Ile mone my selfe, and hide the wrong I haue:
And so content me that her frownes should be
To my' infant stile the cradle, and the graue.

    What though my selfe no honor get thereby,
    Each byrd sings t'herselfe, and so will I.

Sonnet
L.

Loe heere the impost of a faith vnfaining,
That loue hath paide, and her disdaine extorted:
Beholde the message of my iust complayning,
That shewes the world how much my griefe imported.

These tributary plaintes fraught with desire,
I sende those eyes the cabinets of loue;
The Paradice whereto my hopes aspire,
From out this hell, which mine afflictions proue.

Wherein I thus doe liue cast downe from myrth,
Pensiue alone, none but despayre about mee;
My ioyes abortiue, perisht at their byrth,
My cares long liu'de, and will not dye without mee.
  This is my state, and *Delias* hart is such;
  I say no more, I feare I saide too much.

FINIS.

An Ode.

Nowe each creature ioyes the other,
 Passing happy daies and howers:
One byrd reports vnto another,
 In the fall of siluer showers,
Whilst the earth our common mother,
 Hath her bosome deckt with flowers.

Whilst the greatest torch of heauen,
 With bright rayes warmes *Floras* lappe:
Making nights and dayes both euen,
 Cheering plants with fresher sappe:
My field of flowers quite be-reauen,
 Wants refresh of better happe.

Eccho daughter of the ayre,
 Babbling gheste of Rocks and Hills,
Knowes the name of my fearce Fayre,
 And soundes the accents of my ills:
Each thing pitties my dispaire,
 Whilst that she her Louer kills.

Whilst that she O cruell Maide,
 Doth me, and my true loue dispise:
My liues florish is decayde
 That depended on her eyes:
But her will must be obaide,
 And well he'ends for loue who dies.

FINIS.

IDEAS
MIRROVR.

AMOVRS
IN QVATORZAINS.

Che ſerue é tace aſſai domanda.

AT LONDON,
Printed by *Iames Roberts*, for *Nicholas*
Linge. Anno. 1594.

TO THE DEERE CHYLD OF THE MUSES,
AND HIS EVER KIND MECÆNAS,
MA. ANTHONY COOKE,
ESQUIRE.

VOUCHSAFE to grace these rude unpolish'd rymes,
    Which long (deer friend) have slept in sable night,
    And come abroad now in these glorious tymes,
    Can hardly brooke the purenes of the light.

But sith you see their desteny is such,
    That in the world theyr fortune they must try,
    Perhaps they better shall abide the tuch,
    Wearing your name theyr gracious livery.

Yet these mine owne, I wrong not other men,
    Nor trafique further then thys happy Clyme,
    Nor filch from *Portes* nor from *Petrarchs* pen,
    A fault too common in thys latter tyme.
Divine Syr *Phillip,* I avouch thy writ,
I am no Pickpurse of anothers wit.

                Yours devoted,

                    M. Drayton.

ANKOR tryumph, upon whose blessed shore,
    The sacred Muses solemnize thy name:
    Where the *Arcadian* Swaines with rytes adore
    Pandoras poesy, and her living fame.

Where first this jolly Sheepheard gan rehearse,
    That heavenly worth, upon his Oaten reede,
    Of earths great Queene: in Nectar-dewed verse,
    Which none so wise that rightly can areede.

Nowe in conceite of his ambitious love,
    He mounts his thoughts unto the highest gate,
    Straynd with some sacred spirit from above,
    Bewraies his love, his fayth, his life, his fate:

In this his myrror of *Ideas* praise,
    On whom his thoughts, and fortunes all attend,
    Tunes all his Ditties, and his Roundelaies,
    How love begun, how love shal never end.
No wonder though his Muse then soare so hie,
Whose subject is the Queene of Poesie.

Gorbo il fidele.

READE heere (sweet Mayd) the story of my wo,
    The drery abstracts of my endles cares:
    With my lives sorow enterlyned so,
    Smok'd with my sighes, and blotted with my teares.

The sad memorials of my miseries,
    Pend in the griefe of myne afflicted ghost:
    My lives complaint in doleful Elegies,
    With so pure love as tyme could never boast.

Receave the incense which I offer heere,
    By my strong fayth ascending to thy fame,
    My zeale, my hope, my vowes, my praise, my prayer,
    My soules oblations to thy sacred name.
Which name my Muse to highest heaven shal raise,
By chast desire, true love, and vertues praise.

MY FAYRE, if thou wilt register my love,
    More then worlds volumes shall thereof arise,
    Preserve my teares, and thou thy selfe shalt prove
    A second flood downe rayning from mine eyes.

Note but my sighes, and thine eyes shal behold,
    The Sun-beames smothered with immortall smoke:
    And if by thee my prayers may be enrold,
    They heaven and earth to pitty shall provoke.

Looke thou into my breast, and thou shalt see
    Chaste holy vowes for my soules sacrifice:
    That soule (sweet Maide) which so hath honored thee,
    Erecting Trophies to thy sacred eyes.
Those eyes to my hart shining ever bright,
When darknes hath obscur'd each other light.

AMOUR. 3.

MY THOUGHTS bred up with Eagle-birds of love,
    And for their vertues I desierd to know,
    Upon the nest I set them, forth to prove,
    If they were of the Eagles kinde or no.

But they no sooner saw my Sunne appeare,
    But on her rayes with gazing eyes they stood,
    Which proov'd my birds delighted in the ayre,
    And that they came of this rare kinglie brood.

But now their plumes full sumd with sweet desire,
    To shew their kinde, began to clime the skies:
    Doe what I could my Eaglets would aspire,
    Straight mounting up to thy celestiall eyes.
And thus (my faire) my thoughts away be flowne,
And from my breast into thine eyes be gone.

AMOUR. 4.

MY FAIRE, had I not erst adornd my Lute,
    With those sweet strings stolne from thy golden hayre,
    Unto the world had all my joyes been mute,
    Nor had I learn'd to descant on my faire.

Had not mine eye seene thy Celestiall eye,
    Nor my hart knowne the power of thy name,
    My soule had ne'r felt thy Divinitie,
    Nor my Muse been the trumpet of thy fame.

But thy divine perfections by their skill,
    This miracle on my poore Muse have tried:
    And by inspiring, glorifide my quill,
    And in my verse thy selfe art deified.
Thus from thy selfe the cause is thus derived,
That by thy fame all fame shall be survived.

AMOUR. 5.

SINCE holy Vestall lawes have been neglected,
    The Gods pure fire hath been extinguisht quite:
    No Virgine once attending on that light,
    Nor yet those heavenly secrets once respected.

Till thou alone to pay the heavens their dutie,
    Within the Temple of thy sacred name,
    With thine eyes kindling that Celestial flame,
    By those reflecting Sun-beames of thy beautie.

Here Chastity that Vestall most divine,
    Attends that Lampe with eye which never sleepeth,
    The volumes of Religions lawes shee keepeth,
    Making thy breast that sacred reliques shryne,
Where blessed Angels singing day and night,
Praise him which made that fire, which lends that light.

AMOUR. 6.

IN ONE whole world is but one Phœnix found,
    A Phœnix thou, this Phœnix then alone,
    By thy rare plume thy kind is easly knowne,
    With heavenly colours dide, with natures wonder cround,

Heape thine own vertues seasoned by their sunne,
    On heavenlie top of thy divine desire:
    Then with thy beautie set the same on fire,
    So by thy death, thy life shall be begunne.

Thy selfe thus burned in this sacred flame,
    With thine owne sweetnes al the heavens perfuming,
    And stil increasing as thou art consuming,
    Shalt spring againe from th'ashes of thy fame;
And mounting up, shalt to the heavens ascend,
So maist thou live, past world, past fame, past end.

AMOUR. 7.

STAY, stay, sweet Time, behold or ere thou passe
　　From world to world, thou long hast sought to see,
　　That wonder now wherein all wonders be,
　　Where heaven beholds her in a mortall glasse.

Nay, looke thee Time in this Celestiall glasse,
　　And thy youth past, in this faire mirror see:
　　Behold worlds Beautie in her infancie,
　　What shee was then, and thou or ere shee was.

Now passe on Time, to after-worlds tell this,
　　Tell truelie Time what in thy time hath beene,
　　That they may tel more worlds what Time hath seene,
　　And heaven may joy to think on past worlds blisse.
Heere make a Period Time, and saie for mee,
She was, the like that never was, nor never more shalbe.

AMOUR. 8.

UNTO the World, to Learning, and to Heaven,
　　Three nines there are, to everie one a nine,
　　One number of the earth, the other both divine,
　　One wonder woman now makes three od numbers even.

Nine orders first of Angels be in heaven,
　　Nine Muses doe with learning still frequent:
　　These with the Gods are ever resident:
　　Nine worthy men unto the world were given.

My Worthie, one to these nine Worthies, addeth,
　　And my faire Muse, one Muse unto the nine:
　　And my good Angell in my soule divine,
　　With one more order, these nine orders gladdeth.
My Muse, my Worthy, and my Angell then,
Makes every one of these three nines a ten.

AMOUR. 9.

BEAUTY sometime in all her glory crowned,
  Passing by that cleere fountaine of thine eye:
  Her sun-shine face there chaunsing to espy,
  Forgot herselfe, and thought she had been drowned.

And thus whilst Beautie on her beauty gazed,
  Who then yet living, deemd she had been dying,
  And yet in death, some hope of life espying,
  At her own rare perfections so amazed;

Twixt joy and griefe, yet with a smyling frowning,
  The glorious sun-beames of her eyes bright shining,
  And shee on her owne destiny divining,
  Threw in herselfe, to save herselfe by drowning.
The Well of Nectar, pav'd with pearle and gold,
Where shee remaines for all eyes to behold.

AMOUR. 10.

OFT taking pen in hand, with words to cast my woes,
  Beginning to account the sum of all my cares,
  I well perceive my griefe innumerable growes,
  And styll in reckonings rise more millions of dispayres.

And thus deviding of my fatall howres,
  The payments of my love I read, and reading crosse,
  And in substracting, set my sweets unto my sowres,
  Th'arerage of my joyes, directs me to my losse.

And thus mine eyes, a debtor to thine eye,
  Who by extortion gaineth all theyr lookes,
  My hart hath payd such grievous usury,
  That all her wealth lyes in thy Beauties bookes.
And all is thine which hath been due to mee,
And I a Banckrupt quite undone by thee.

AMOUR. 11.

THINE eyes taught mee the Alphabet of love,
    To con my Cros-rowe ere I learn'd to spell:
    For I was apt a scholler like to prove,
    Gave mee sweet lookes when as I learned well.

Vowes were my vowels when I then begun
    At my first Lesson in thy sacred name,
    My consonants the next when I had done,
    Words consonant, and sounding to thy fame.

My liquids then were liquid christall teares,
    My cares my mutes so mute to crave reliefe,
    My dolefull Dypthongs were my lives dispaires,
    Redoubling sighes the accents of my griefe:
My loves Schoole-mistris now hath taught me so,
That I can reade a story of my woe.

AMOUR. 12.

SOME Athiest or vile Infidell in love,
    When I doe speake of thy divinitie,
    May blaspheme thus, and say, I flatter thee:
    And onely write, my skill in verse to prove.

See myracles, yee unbeleeving see,
    A dumbe-borne Muse made to expresse the mind,
    A cripple hand to write, yet lame by kind,
    One by thy name, the other touching thee.

Blind were mine eyes, till they were seene of thine,
    And mine eares deafe, by thy fame healed be,
    My vices cur'd, by vertues sprung from thee,
    My hopes reviv'd which long in grave had lyne.
All uncleane thoughts, foule spirits cast out in mee,
By thy great power, and by strong fayth in thee.

AMOUR. 13.

CLEERE *Ankor,* on whose silver-sanded shore,
   My soule-shrinde Saint, my faire *Idea* lyes:
   O blessed Brooke, whose milk-white Swans adore
   That christall streame refined by her eyes.

Where sweet Myrh-breathing *Zephyre* in the spring,
   Gently distils his Nectar-dropping showers:
   Where Nightingals in *Arden* sit and sing,
   Amongst those dainty dew-empearled flowers.

Say thus fayre Brooke when thou shalt see thy Queene,
   Loe, heere thy Shepheard spent his wandring yeeres:
   And in these shades (deer Nimphe) he oft hath been,
   And heere to thee he sacrifiz'd his teares.
Fayre *Arden,* thou my *Tempe* art alone,
And thou sweet *Ankor* art my *Helicon.*

AMOUR. 14.

LOOKING into the glasse of my youths miseries,
   I see the ugly face of my deformed cares,
   With withered browes, all wrinckled with dispaires,
   That for my mis-spent youth the tears fel from my eyes.

Then in these teares, the mirrors of these eyes,
   Thy fayrest youth and Beautie doe I see,
   Imprinted in my teares by looking still on thee:
   Thus midst a thousand woes, ten thousand joyes arise.

Yet in these joyes, the shadowes of my good,
   In this fayre limmed ground as white as snow,
   Paynted the blackest Image of my woe,
   With murthering hands imbrud in mine own blood.
And in thys Image his darke clowdy eyes,
My life, my youth, my love, I heere Anotamize.

AMOUR. 15.

NOW love, if thou wilt prove a Conqueror,
     Subdue thys Tyrant ever martyring mee,
     And but appoint me for her Tormentor,
     Then for a Monarch will I honour thee.

My hart shall be the prison for my fayre,
     Ile fetter her in chaines of purest love,
     My sighes shall stop the passage of the ayre:
     This punishment the pittilesse may move.

With teares out of the Channels of mine eyes,
     She'st quench her thirst as duly as they fall:
     Kinde words unkindest meate I can devise,
     My sweet, my faire, my good, my best of all.

Ile binde her then with my torne-tressed haire,
     And racke her with a thousand holy wishes,
     Then on a place prepared for her there,
     Ile execute her with a thousand kisses.
Thus will I crucifie my cruell shee,
Thus Ile plague her which so hath plagued mee.

AMOUR. 16.

VERTUES *Idea* in virginitie,
     By inspiration, came conceav'd with thought:
     The time is come delivered she must be,
     Where first my Love into the world was brought.

Unhappy Borne, of all unhappy day,
     So luckles was my Babes nativity:
     Saturne chiefe Lord of the Ascendant lay,
     The wandring Moone in earths triplicitie.

Now, or by chaunce, or heavens hie providence,
     His Mother died, and by her Legacie,
     (Fearing the stars presaged influence,)
     Bequeath'd his wardship to my soveraignes eye;

Where hunger-starven, wanting lookes to live,
  Still empty gorg'd, with cares consumption pynde,
  Salt luke-warme teares shee for his drinke did give,
  And ever-more with sighes he supt and dynde.
And thus (poore Orphan) lying in distresse,
Cryes in his pangs, God helpe the motherlesse.

AMOUR. 17.

IF EVER wonder could report a wonder,
  Or tongue of wonder worth could tell a wonder thought,
  Or ever joy expresse, what perfect joy hath taught,
  Then wonder, tongue, then joy, might wel report a wonder.

Could all conceite conclude, which past conceite admireth,
  Or could mine eye but ayme, her objects past perfection,
  My words might imitate my deerest thoughts direction:
  And my soule then obtaine which so my soule desireth.

Were not Invention stauld, treading Inventions maze,
  Or my swift-winged Muse tyred by too hie flying,
  Did not perfection still on her perfection gaze,
  Whilst Love (my Phœnix bird) in her own flame is dying,
Invention and my Muse, perfection and her love,
Should teach the world to know the wonder that I prove.

AMOUR. 18.

SOME when in ryme they of their Loves doe tell,
  With flames and lightning their exordiums paynt,
  Some invocate the Gods, some spirits of Hell,
  And heaven, and earth, doe with their woes acquaint.

Elizia is too hie a seate for mee,
  I wyll not come in *Stixe* nor *Phlegiton,*
  The Muses nice, the Furies cruell be,
  I lyke not *Limbo,* nor blacke *Acheron,*

Spightfull *Errinis* frights mee with her lookes,
  My manhood dares not with foule *Ate* mell,
  I quake to looke on *Hecats* charming bookes,

I styll feare bugbeares in *Apollos* Cell.
I passe not for *Minerva* nor *Astraea*,
But ever call upon divine *Idea*.

AMOUR. 19.

I F THOSE ten Regions registred by Fame,
    By theyr ten Sibils have the world controld,
    Who prophecied of Christ or ere he came,
    And of hys blessed birth before fore-told.

That man-god now of whom they dyd divine,
    This earth of those sweet Prophets hath bereft,
    And since the world to judgement doth declyne,
    In steed of ten, one Sibil to us left.

Thys, pure *Idea*, vertues right *Idea*,
    Shee of whom *Merlin* long tyme did fore-tell,
    Excelling her of *Delphos* or *Cumaea*,
    Whose lyfe doth save a thousand soules from hell:
That life (I meane) which doth Religion teach,
And by example, true repentance preach.

AMOUR. 20.

READING sometyme, my sorrowes to beguile,
    I find old Poets hylls and floods admire.
    One, he doth wonder monster-breeding *Nyle*,
    Another, mervailes Sulphure *Aetnas* fire.

Now broad-brymd *Indus*, then of *Pindus* height,
    Pelion and *Ossa*, frosty *Caucase* old,
    The Delian *Cynthus*, then *Olympus* weight,
    Slow *Arrer*, frantick *Gallus*, *Cydnus* cold.

Some *Ganges*, *Ister*, and of *Tagus* tell,
    Some whir-poole *Po*, and slyding *Hypasis*,
    Some old *Pernassus*, where the Muses dwell,
    Some *Helycon*, and some faire *Simois*,
A fooles thinke I, had you *Idea* seene,
Poore Brookes and Banks had no such wonders beene.

LETTERS and lynes we see are soone defaced,
 Mettles doe waste, and fret with cankers rust,
 The Diamond shall once consume to dust,
 And freshest colours with foule staines disgraced.

Paper and yncke, can paynt but naked words,
 To write with blood, of force offends the sight,
 And if with teares, I find them all too light:
 And sighes and signes a silly hope affoords.

O sweetest shadow, how thou serv'st my turne,
 Which still shalt be as long as there is Sunne,
 Nor whilst the world is, never shall be done,
 Whilst Moone shall shyne by night, or any fire shall burne.
That every thing whence shadow doth proceede,
May in his shadow my Loves story reade.

MY HART imprisoned in a hopeles Ile,
 Peopled with Armies of pale jealous eyes,
 The shores beset with thousand secret spyes,
 Must passe by ayre, or else dye in exile.

He framd him wings with feathers of his thought,
 Which by theyr nature learn'd to mount the skye,
 And with the same he practised to flye,
 Till he himselfe thys Eagles art had taught.

Thus soring still, not looking once below,
 So neere thyne eyes celestiall sunne aspyred,
 That with the rayes his wafting pyneons fired.
 Thus was the wanton cause of hys owne woe.
Downe fell he in thy Beauties Ocean drenched,
Yet there he burnes, in fire thats never quenched.

AMOUR. 23.

WONDER of Heaven, glasse of divinitie,
  Rare beauty, Natures joy, perfections Mother,
  The worke of that united Trinitie,
  Wherein each fayrest part excelleth other.

Loves Methridate, the purest of perfection,
  Celestiall Image, Load-stone of desire,
  The soules delight, the sences true direction,
  Sunne of the world, thou hart revyving fire.

Why should'st thou place thy Trophies in those eyes,
  Which scorne the honor that is done to thee,
  Or make my pen her name imortalize,
  Who in her pride sdaynes once to looke on mee.

It is thy heaven within her face to dwell,
And in thy heaven, there onely is my hell.

AMOUR. 24.

OUR floods-Queene *Thames,* for shyps & Swans is crowned,
  And stately *Severne,* for her shores is praised,
  The christall *Trent,* for Foords & fishe renowned,
  And *Avons* fame, to *Albyons* Clives is raysed.

Carlegion Chester, vaunts her holy *Dee,*
  Yorke, many wonders of her *Ouse* can tell,
  The *Peake* her *Dove,* whose bancks so fertill bee,
  And *Kent* will say, her *Medway* doth excell.

Cotswoold commends her *Isis* and her *Tame,*
  Our Northern borders boast of *Tweeds* faire flood,
  Our Westerne parts extoll theyr *Wilys* fame,
  And old *Legea* brags of *Danish* blood:

Ardens sweet *Ankor* let thy glory be,
That fayre *Idea* shee doth live by thee.

AMOUR. 25.

THE glorious sunne went blushing to his bed,
  When my soules sunne from her fayre Cabynet,
  Her golden beames had now discovered,
  Lightning the world, eclipsed by his set.

Some muz'd to see the earth envy the ayre,
  Which from her lyps exhald refined sweet,
  A world to see, yet how he joyd to heare
  The dainty grasse make musicke with her feete.

But my most mervaile was when from the skyes,
  So Comet-like each starre advaunc'd her lyght,
  As though the heaven had now awak'd her eyes,
  And summond Angels to thys blessed sight.
No clowde was seene, but christaline the ayre,
Laughing for joy upon my lovely fayre.

AMOUR. 26.

CUPID, dumbe Idoll, peevish Saint of love,
  No more shalt thou nor Saint nor Idoll be,
  No God art thou, a Goddesse shee doth prove,
  Of all thine honour shee hath robbed thee.

Thy Bowe halfe broke, is peec'd with olde desire,
  Her Bowe is beauty, with ten thousand strings,
  Of purest gold, tempred with vertues fire:
  The least able to kyll an hoste of Kings.

Thy shafts be spent, and shee (to warre appointed)
  Hydes in those christall quivers of her eyes,
  More Arrowes with hart-piercing mettel poynted,
  Then there be starres at midnight in the skyes.
With these, she steales mens harts for her reliefe,
Yet happy he thats robd of such a thiefe.

104

AMOUR. 27.

MY LOVE makes hote the fire whose heat is spent,
　　The water, moysture from my teares deriveth:
　　And my strong sighes, the ayres weake force reviveth.
　　This love, tears, sighes, maintaine each one his element.

The fire, unto my love, compare a painted fire,
　　The water, to my teares, as drops to Oceans be,
　　The ayre, unto my sighes, as Eagle to the flie,
　　The passions of dispaire, but joyes to my desire.

Onely my love is in the fire ingraved,
　　Onely my teares by Oceans may be gessed,
　　Onely my sighes are by the ayre expressed,
　　Yet fire, water, ayre, of nature not deprived.
Whilst fire, water, ayre, twixt heaven & earth shal be,
My love, my teares, my sighes, extinguisht cannot be.

AMOUR. 28.

SOME wits there be, which lyke my method well,
　　And say my verse runnes in a lofty vayne,
　　Some say I have a passing pleasing straine,
　　Some say that in my humor I excell.

Some, who reach not the height of my conceite,
　　They say, (as Poets doe) I use to fayne,
　　And in bare words paynt out my passions payne.
　　Thus sundry men, their sundry minds repeate.

I passe not I how men affected be,
　　Nor who commend or discommend my verse,
　　It pleaseth me if I my plaints rehearse,
　　And in my lynes if shee my love may see.
I prove my verse autentique still in thys,
Who writes my Mistres praise, can never write amisse.

AMOUR. 29.

O EYES, behold your happy *Hesperus,*
    That luckie Load-starre of eternall light,
    Left as that sunne alone to comfort us,
    When our worlds sunne is vanisht out of sight.

O starre of starres, fayre Planet mildly mooving,
    O Lampe of vertue, sun-bright, ever shyning,
    O mine eyes Comet, so admyr'd by loving,
    O cleerest day-starre, never more declyning.

O our worlds wonder, crowne of heaven above,
    Thrice happy be those eyes which may behold thee,
    Lov'd more then life, yet onely art his love,
    Whose glorious hand immortall hath enrold thee.
O blessed fayre, now vaile those heavenly eyes,
That I may blesse mee at thy sweet arise.

AMOUR. 30.

THREE sorts of Serpents doe resemble thee,
    That daungerous eye-killing Cockatrice,
    Th'inchaunting Syren, which doth so entice,
    The weeping Crocodile: these vile pernicious three.

The Basiliske his nature takes from thee,
    Who for my life in secrete waite do'st lye,
    And to my hart send'st poyson from thine eye,
    Thus do I feele the paine, the cause, yet cannot see.

Faire-mayd no more, but Mayr-maid be thy name,
    Who with thy sweet aluring harmony
    Hast playd the thiefe, and stolne my hart from me,
    And like a Tyrant mak'st my griefe thy game.
Thou Crocodile, who when thou hast me slaine,
Lament'st my death, with teares of thy disdaine.

AMOUR. 31.

SITTING alone, love bids me goe and write,
    Reason plucks backe, commaunding me to stay,
    Boasting that shee doth still direct the way,
    Els senceles love could never once endite.

Love growing angry, vexed at the spleene,
    And scorning Reasons maymed Argument,
    Straight taxeth Reason, wanting to invent,
    Where shee with Love conversing hath not beene.

Reason reproched with this coy disdaine,
    Dispighteth Love, and laugheth at her folly,
    And Love contemning Reasons reason wholy,
    Thought her in weight too light by many a graine.
Reason put back, doth out of sight remove,
And Love alone finds reason in my love.

AMOUR. 32.

THOSE teares which quench my hope, still kindle my desire,
    Those sighes which coole my hart, are coles unto my love,
    Disdayne Ice to my life, is to my soule a fire,
    With teares, sighes, & disdaine, thys contrary I prove.

Quenchles desire, makes hope burne, dryes my teares,
    Love heats my hart, my hart-heat my sighes warmeth,
    With my soules fire, my life disdaine out-weares,
    Desire, my love, my soule, my hope, hart, & life charmeth.

My hope becomes a friend to my desire,
    My hart imbraceth Love, Love doth imbrace my hart,
    My life a Phœnix is in my soules fire,
    From thence (they vow) they never will depart.
Desire, my love, my soule, my hope, my hart, my life,
With teares, sighes, and disdaine, shall have immortal strife.

AMOUR. 33.

WHILST thus mine eyes doe surfet with delight,
　　My wofull hart imprisond in my breast,
　　Wishing to be trans-formd into my sight,
　　To looke on her by whom mine eyes are blest.

But whilst mine eyes thus greedily doe gaze,
　　Behold, their objects over-soone depart,
　　And treading in thys never-ending maze,
　　Wish now to be trans-formd into my hart.

My hart surcharg'd with thoughts, sighes in abundance raise,
　　My eyes made dim with lookes, poure down a flood of tears,
　　And whilst my hart and eye, envy each others praise,
　　My dying lookes and thoughts are peiz'd in equall feares.
And thus whilst sighes and teares together doe contende,
Each one of these, doth ayde unto the other lende.

AMOUR. 34.

MY FAYRE, looke from those turrets of thine eyes,
　　Into the Ocean of a troubled minde,
　　Where my poore soule, the Barke of sorrow lyes,
　　Left to the mercy of the waves and winde.

See where shee flotes, laden with purest love,
　　Which those fayre Ilands of thy lookes affoord,
　　Desiring yet a thousand deaths to prove,
　　Then so to cast her Ballast over boord.

See how her sayles be rent, her tacklings worne,
　　Her Cable broke, her surest Anchor lost,
　　Her Marryners doe leave her all forlorne,
　　Yet how shee bends towards that blessed Coast.
Loe where she drownes, in stormes of thy displeasure,
Whose worthy prize should have enritcht thy treasure.

SEE chaste *Diana,* where my harmles hart,
    Rouz'd from my breast, his sure and safest layre,
    Nor chaste by hound, nor forc'd by Hunters arte,
    Yet see how right he comes unto my fayre.

See how my Deere comes to thy Beauties stand,
    And there stands gazing on those darting eyes,
    Whilst from theyr rayes by *Cupids* skilfull hand,
    Into his hart the piercing Arrow flyes.

See how hee lookes upon his bleeding wound,
    Whilst thus he panteth for his latest breath,
    And looking on thee, falls upon the ground,
    Smyling, as though he gloried in his death.
And wallowing in his blood, some lyfe yet laft,
His stone-cold lips doth kisse the blessed shaft.

SWEETE sleepe so arm'd with Beauties arrowes darting,
    Sleepe in thy Beauty, Beauty in sleepe appeareth,
    Sleepe lightning Beauty, Beauty sleepes darknes cleereth,
    Sleepes wonder Beauty, wonders to worlds imparting.

Sleep watching Beauty, Beauty waking, sleepe guarding,
    Beauty in sleepe, sleepe in Beauty charmed,
    Sleepes aged coldnes, with Beauties fire warmed,
    Sleepe with delight, Beauty with love rewarding.

Sleepe and Beauty, with equall forces stryving,
    Beauty her strength unto sleepes weaknes lending,
    Sleepe with Beauty, Beauty with sleepe contending,
    Yet others force, the others force reviving:
And others foe, the others foe imbrace,
Myne eyes beheld thys conflict in thy face.

I EVER love, where never hope appeares,
    Yet hope drawes on my never-hoping care,
    And my lives hope would die but for dyspaire,
    My never certaine joy, breeds ever-certaine feares.

Uncertaine-dread, gyves wings unto my hope,
    Yet my hopes wings are loden so with feare,
    As they cannot ascend to my hopes spheare,
    Yet feare gyves them more then a heavenly scope:

Yet thys large roome is bounded with dyspaire,
    So my love is styll fettered with vaine hope,
    And lyberty deprives hym of hys scope,
    And thus am I imprisond in the ayre;
Then sweet Dispaire, a while hold up thy head,
Or all my hope for sorrow will be dead.

IF CHASTE and pure devotion of my youth,
    Or glorie of my Aprill-springing yeeres,
    Unfained love, in naked simple truth,
    A thousand vowes, a thousand sighes and teares:

Or if a world of faithfull service done,
    Words, thoughts, and deeds, devoted to her honor,
    Or eyes that have beheld her as theyr sunne,
    With admiration, ever looking on her.

A lyfe, that never joyd but in her love,
    A soule, that ever hath ador'd her name,
    A fayth, that time nor fortune could not move,
    A Muse, that unto heaven hath raisd her fame.
Though these, nor these, deserve to be imbraced,
Yet faire unkinde, too good to be disgraced.

AMOUR. 39.

DIE, die, my soule, and never taste of joy,
  If sighes, nor teares, nor vowes, nor prayers can move,
  If fayth and zeale be but esteemd a toy,
  And kindnes, be unkindnes in my love.

Then with unkindnes, Love revenge thy wrong,
  O sweet'st revenge that ere the heavens gave,
  And with the Swan record thy dying song,
  And praise her still to thy untimely grave.

So in loves death shall loves perfection prove,
  That love divine which I have borne to you,
  By doome concealed to the heavens above,
  That yet the world unworthy never knewe,
Whose pure *Idea* never tongue exprest,
I feele, you know, the heavens can tell the rest.

AMOUR. 40.

O THOU unkindest fayre, most fayrest shee,
  In thine eyes tryumph murthering my poore hart,
  Now doe I sweare by heavens, before we part,
  My halfe-slaine hart shall take revenge on thee.

Thy Mother dyd her lyfe to Death resigne,
  And thou an Angell art, and from above,
  Thy father was a man, that will I prove,
  Yet thou a Goddesse art, and so divine.

And thus if thou be not of humaine kinde,
  A Bastard on both sides needes must thou be,
  Our Lawes alow no Land to basterdy:
  By natures Lawes we thee a Bastard finde.
Then hence to heaven unkind, for thy childs part,
Goe Bastard goe, for sure of thence thou art.

AMOUR. 41.

RARE of-spring of my thoughts, my deerest Love,
    Begot by fancy, on sweet hope exhortive,
    In whom all purenes with perfection strove,
    Hurt in the Embryon, makes my joyes abhortive.

And you my sighes, Symtomas of my woe,
    The dolefull Anthems of my endlesse care,
    Lyke idle Ecchoes ever aunswering: so,
    The mournfull accents of my loves dispayre.

And thou Conceite, the shadow of my blisse,
    Declyning with the setting of my sunne,
    Springing with that, and fading straight with this,
    Now hast thou end, and now thou wast begun.
Now was thy pryme, and loe, now is thy waine,
Now wast thou borne, now in thy cradle slayne.

AMOUR. 42.

PLAC'D in the forlorne hope of all dispayre,
    Against the Forte where Beauties Army lies,
    Assayld with death, yet arm'd with gastly feare,
    Loe thus my love, my lyfe, my fortune tryes.

Wounded with Arrowes from thy lightning eyes,
    My tongue in payne, my harts counsels bewraying,
    My rebell thought for me in Ambushe lyes,
    To my lyves foe her Chieftaine still betraying.

Record my love in Ocean waves (unkind,)
    Cast my desarts into the open ayre,
    Commit my words unto the fleeting wind,
    Cancell my name, and blot it with dispayre,
So shall I be, as I had never beene,
Nor my disgraces to the world be seene.

AMOUR. 43.

WHY doe I speake of joy, or write of love,
    When my hart is the very Den of horror,
    And in my soule the paynes of hell I prove,
    With all his torments and infernall terror.

Myne eyes want teares thus to bewayle my woe,
    My brayne is dry with weeping all too long,
    My sighes be spent with griefe and sighing so,
    And I want words for to expresse my wrong.

But still distracted in loves Lunacy,
    And Bedlam like thus raving in my griefe,
    Now rayle upon her hayre, now on her eye,
    Now call her Goddesse, then I call her thiefe,
Now I deny her, then I doe confesse her,
Now doe I curse her, then againe I blesse her.

AMOUR. 44.

MY HART the Anvile where my thoughts doe beate,
    My words the hammers, fashioning my desires,
    My breast the forge, including all the heate,
    Love is the fuell which maintaines the fire.

My sighes, the bellowes which the flame increaseth,
    Filling myne eares with noyse and nightly groning,
    Toyling with paine, my labour never ceaseth,
    In greevous passions my woes styll bemoning.

Myne eyes with teares against the fire stryving,
    With scorching gleed my hart to cynders turneth:
    But with those drops the coles againe revyving,
    Still more and more unto my torment burneth.
With *Sisiphus* thus doe I role the stone,
And turne the wheele with damned *Ixion.*

AMOUR. 45.

BLACKE pytchy Night, companyon of my woe,
  The Inne of care, the Nurse of drery sorrow,
  Why lengthnest thou thy darkest howres so,
  Still to prolong my long tyme lookt-for morrow?

Thou Sable shadow, Image of dispayre,
  Portraite of hell, the ayres black mourning weed,
  Recorder of revenge, remembrancer of care,
  The shadow and the vaile of every sinfull deed.

Death like to thee, so lyve thou still in death,
  The grave of joy, pryson of dayes delight,
  Let heavens withdraw their sweet Ambrozian breath,
  Nor Moone nor stars lend thee their shining light.
For thou alone renew'st that olde desire,
Which still torments me in dayes burning fire.

AMOUR. 46.

SWEET secrecie, what tongue can tell thy worth?
  What mortall pen suffyciently can prayse thee?
  What curious Pensill serves to lim thee forth?
  What Muse hath power, above thy height to raise thee?

Strong locke of kindnesse, Closet of loves store,
  Harts Methridate, the soules preservative,
  O vertue, which all vertues doe adore,
  Cheefe good, from whom all good things we derive.

O rare effect, true bond of friendships measure,
  Conceite of Angels, which all wisdom teachest,
  O richest Casket of all heavenly treasure,
  In secret silence, which such wonders preachest,
O purest merror, wherein men may see
The lively Image of Divinitie.

AMOUR. 47.

THE golden Sunne upon his fiery wheeles,
    The horned Ram doth in his course a wake:
    And of just length our night and day doth make,
    Flinging the Fishes backward with his heeles.

    Then to the Tropicke takes his full Careere,
    Trotting his sun-steeds till the Palfrays sweat,
    Bayting the Lyon in his furious heat,
    Till Virgins smyles doe sound his sweet reteere.

But my faire Planet, who directs me still,
    Unkindly, such distemprature doth bring,
    Makes Summer Winter, Autumne in the Spring,
    Crossing sweet nature by unruly will.
Such is the sunne, who guides my youthfull season,
Whose thwarting course, deprives the world of reason.

AMOUR. 48.

WHO list to praise the dayes delicious lyght,
    Let him compare it to her heavenly eye:
    The sun-beames to that lustre of her sight,
    So may the learned like the similie.

The mornings Crimson, to her lyps alike,
    The sweet of *Eden,* to her breathes perfume,
    The fayre *Elizia,* to her fayrer cheeke,
    Unto her veynes, the onely Phœnix plume.

The Angels tresses, to her tressed hayre,
    The *Galixia,* to her more then white:
    Praysing the fayrest, compare it to my faire,
    Still naming her, in naming all delight.
So may he grace all these in her alone,
Superlative in all comparison.

DEFINE my love, and tell the joyes of heaven,
    Expresse my woes, and shew the paynes of hell,
    Declare what fate unlucky starres have given,
    And aske a world upon my life to dwell.

Make knowne that fayth, unkindnes could not move,
    Compare my worth with others base desert,
    Let vertue be the tuch-stone of my love,
    So may the heavens reade wonders in my hart.

Behold the Clowdes which have eclips'd my sunne,
    And view the crosses which my course doth let,
    Tell mee, if ever since the world begunne,
    So faire a Morning had so foule a set?
And by all meanes, let black unkindnes prove,
The patience of so rare divine a love.

WHEN first I ended, then I first began,
    The more I travell, further from my rest,
    Where most I lost, there most of all I wan,
    Pyned with hunger, rysing from a feast.

Mee thinks I flee, yet want I legs to goe,
    Wise in conceite, in acte a very sot,
    Ravisht with joy, amidst a hell of woe,
    What most I seeme, that surest am I not.

I build my hopes, a world above the skye,
    Yet with the Mole, I creepe into the earth,
    In plenty, am I starv'd with penury,
    And yet I surfet in the greatest dearth.
I have, I want, dispayre, and yet desire,
Burn'd in a Sea of Ice, & drown'd amidst a fire.

AMOUR. 51.

GOE you my lynes, Embassadors of love,
  With my harts trybute to her conquering eyes,
  From whence, if you one teare of pitty move
  For all my woes, that onely shall suffise.

When you *Minerva* in the sunne behold,
  At her perfection stand you then and gaze,
  Where, in the compasse of a Marygold,
  Meridianis sits within a maze.

And let Invention of her beauty vaunt,
  When *Dorus* sings his sweet *Pamelas* love,
  And tell the Gods, *Mars* is predominant,
  Seated with *Sol,* and weares *Minervas* glove.
And tell the world, that in the world there is
A heaven on earth, on earth no heaven but this.

FINIS.

AMORETTI
AND
Epithalamion.

Written not long since
by Edmunde
Spenser.

Printed for William
Ponsonby. 1595.

To the Right Worship-
full Sir Robart Need-
ham Knight.

 Ir, to gratulate your safe return from Ireland, I had nothing so readie, nor thought any thing so meete, as these sweete conceited Sonets, the deede of that weldeseruing gentleman, maister Edmond Spenser: whose name sufficiently warranting the worthinesse of the work: I do more confidently presume to publish it in his absence, vnder your name to whom (in my poore opinion) the patronage therof, doth in some respectes properly appertaine. For, besides your iudgement and delighte in learned poesie: This gentle Muse for her former perfection long wished for in Englande, nowe at the length crossing the Seas in your happy companye, (though to your selfe vnknowne) seemeth to make choyse of you, as meetest to giue her deserued countenaunce, after her retourne: entertaine her, then, (Right worshipfull) in sorte best beseeming your gentle minde, and her merite, and take in worth my good will herein, who seeke no more, but to shew my selfe yours in all dutifull affection.

W. P.

G: W. senior, to the Author

DArke is the day, when *Phœbus* face is shrowded,
   and weaker sights may wander soone astray:
   but when they see his glorious raies vnclowded,
   with steddy steps they keepe the perfect way:
So while this Muse in forraine landes doth stay,
   Inuention weepes, and pens are cast aside,
   the time like night, depriud of chearefull day,
   and few do write, but (ah) too soone may slide. '
Then, hie thee home, that art our perfect guide,
   and with thy wit illustrate Englands fame,
   dawnting thereby our neighboures auncient pride,
   that do for poesie, challendge cheefest name.
So we that liue and ages that succeede,
   With great applause thy learned works shall reede.

Ah Colin, whether on the lowly plaine,
   pyping to shepherds thy sweete roundelaies:
   or whether singing in some lofty vaine,
   heroick deedes, of past, or present daies
Or whether in thy louely mistris praise,
   thou list to exercise thy learned quill,
   thy muse hath got such grace, and power to please,
   with rare inuention bewtified by skill,
As who therein can euer ioy their fill.
   O therefore let that happy muse proceede
   to clime the height of vertues sacred hill,
   where endles honor shall be made thy meede.
Because no malice of succeeding daies,
   can rase those records of thy lasting praise.

G. W. I.

SONNET.
I.

HAppy ye leaues when as those lilly hands,
    which hold my life in their dead doing might
    shall handle you and hold in loues soft bands,
    lyke captiues trembling at the victors sight.
And happy lines, on which with starry light,
    those lamping eyes will deigne sometimes to look
    and reade the sorrowes of my dying spright,
    written with teares in harts close bleeding book.
And happy rymes bath'd in the sacred brooke,
    of *Helicon* whence she deriued is,
    when ye behold that Angels blessed looke,
    my soules long lacked foode, my heauens blis.
Leaues, lines, and rymes, seeke her to please alone,
    whom if ye please, I care for other none.

SONNET.
II.

VNquiet thought, whom at the first I bred,
    Of th'inward bale of my loue pined hart:
    and sithens haue with sighes and sorrowes fed,
    till greater then my wombe thou woxen art.
Breake forth at length out of the inner part,
    in which thou lurkest lyke to vipers brood:
    and seeke some succour both to ease my smart
    and also to sustayne thy selfe with food.
But if in presence of that fayrest proud
    thou chance to come, fall lowly at her feet:
    and with meeke humblesse and afflicted mood,
    pardon for thee, and grace for me intreat.
Which if she graunt, then liue and my loue cherish,
    if not, die soone, and I with thee will perish.

SONNET.
III.

THe souerayne beauty which I doo admyre,
    witnesse the world how worthy to be prayzed:
    the light wherof hath kindled heauenly fyre,
    in my fraile spirit by her from basenesse raysed.
That being now with her huge brightnesse dazed,
    base thing I can no more endure to view:
    but looking still on her I stand amazed,
    at wondrous sight of so celestiall hew.

So when my toung would speak her praises dew,
   it stopped is with thoughts astonishment:
   and when my pen would write her titles true,
   it rauisht is with fancies wonderment:
Yet in my hart I then both speake and write
   the wonder that my wit cannot endite.

NEw yeare forth looking out of Ianus gate,
   Doth seeme to promise hope of new delight:
   and bidding th'old Adieu, his passed date
   bids all old thoughts to die in dumpish spright,
And calling forth out of sad Winters night,
   fresh loue, that long hath slept in cheerlesse bower:
   wils him awake, and soone about him dight
   his wanton wings and darts of deadly power.
For lusty spring now in his timely howre,
   is ready to come forth him to receiue:
   and warnes the Earth with diuers colord flowre,
   to decke hir selfe, and her faire mantle weaue.
Then you faire flowre, in whom fresh youth doth raine,
   prepare your selfe new loue to entertaine.

SONNET.
IIII.

RVdely thou wrongest my deare harts desire,
   In finding fault with her too portly pride:
   the thing which I doo most in her admire,
   is of the world vnworthy most enuide.
For in those lofty lookes is close implide,
   scorn of base things, and sdeigne of foule dishonor:
   thretning rash eies which gaze on her so wide,
   that loosely they ne dare to looke vpon her.
Such pride is praise, such portlinesse is honor,
   that boldned innocence beares in hir eies:
   and her faire countenance like a goodly banner,
   spreds in defiaunce of all enemies.
Was neuer in this world ought worthy tride,
   without some spark of such self-pleasing pride.

SONNET.
V.

SONNET.
VI.

BE nought dismayd that her vnmoued mind
    doth still persist in her rebellious pride:
    such loue not lyke to lusts of baser kynd,
    the harder wonne, the firmer will abide.
The durefull Oake, whose sap is not yet dride,
    is long ere it conceiue the kindling fyre:
    but when it once doth burne, it doth diuide
    great heat, and makes his flames to heauen aspire.
So hard it is to kindle new desire,
    in gentle brest that shall endure for euer:
    deepe is the wound, that dints the parts entire
    with chast affects, that naught but death can seuer.
Then thinke not long in taking litle paine,
    to knit the knot, that euer shall remaine.

SONNET.
VII.

FAyre eyes, the myrrour of my mazed hart,
    what wondrous vertue is contaynd in you
    the which both lyfe and death forth from you dart
    into the obiect of your mighty view?
For when ye mildly looke with louely hew,
    then is my soule with life and loue inspired:
    but when ye lowre, or looke on me askew,
    then doe I die, as one with lightning fyred.
But since that lyfe is more then death desyred,
    looke euer louely, as becomes you best,
    that your bright beams of my weak eies admyred,
    may kindle liuing fire within my brest.
Such life should be the honor of your light,
    such death the sad ensample of your might.

SONNET.
VIII.

MOre then most faire, full of the liuing fire,
    Kindled aboue vnto the maker neere:
    no eies but ioyes, in which al powers conspire,
    that to the world naught else be counted deare.
Thrugh your bright beams doth not the blinded guest
    shoot out his darts to base affections wound?
    but Angels come to lead fraile mindes to rest
    in chast desires on heauenly beauty bound.

You frame my thoughts and fashion me within,
    you stop my toung, and teach my hart to speake,
    you calme the storme that passion did begin,
    strong thrugh your cause, but by your vertue weak.
Dark is the world, where your light shined neuer;
    well is he borne, that may behold you euer.

LOng-while I sought to what I might compare
    those powrefull eies, which lighten my dark spright,
    yet find I nought on earth to which I dare
    resemble th'ymage of their goodly light.
Not to the Sun: for they doo shine by night;
    nor to the Moone: for they are changed neuer;
    nor to the Starres: for they haue purer sight;
    nor to the fire: for they consume not euer;
Nor to the lightning: for they still perseuer;
    nor to the Diamond: for they are more tender;
    nor vnto Christall: for nought may them seuer;
    nor vnto glasse: such basenesse mought offend her;
Then to the Maker selfe they likest be,
    whose light doth lighten all that here we see.

VNrighteous Lord of loue what law is this,
    That me thou makest thus tormented be?
    the whiles she lordeth in licentious blisse
    of her freewill, scorning both thee and me.
See how the Tyrannesse doth ioy to see
    the huge massacres which her eyes do make:
    and humbled harts brings captiues vnto thee,
    that thou of them mayst mightie vengeance take.
But her proud hart doe thou a little shake
    and that high look, with which she doth comptroll
    all this worlds pride bow to a baser make,
    and al her faults in thy black booke enroll.
That I may laugh at her in equall sort,
    as she doth laugh at me and makes my pain her sport.

SONNET.
XI.

DAyly when I do seeke and sew for peace,
    And hostages doe offer for my truth:
      she cruell warriour doth her selfe addresse
      to battell, and the weary war renew'th.
Ne wilbe moou'd with reason or with rewth,
    to graunt small respit to my restlesse toile:
      but greedily her fell intent poursewth,
      Of my poore life to make vnpittied spoile.
Yet my poore life, all sorrowes to assoyle,
    I would her yield, her wrath to pacify:
      but then she seekes with torment and turmoyle,
      to force me liue and will not let me dy.
All paine hath end and euery war hath peace,
    but mine no price nor prayer may surcease.

SONNET.
XII.

ONe day I sought with her hart-thrilling eies,
    to make a truce and termes to entertaine:
      all fearelesse then of so false enimies,
      which sought me to entrap in treasons traine.
So as I then disarmed did remaine,
    a wicked ambush which lay hidden long
      in the close couert of her guilefull eyen,
      thence breaking forth did thick about me throng.
Too feeble I t'abide the brunt so strong,
    was forst to yeeld my selfe into their hands:
      who me captiuing streight with rigorous wrong,
      haue euer since me kept in cruell bands.
So Ladie now to you I doo complaine,
    against your eies that iustice I may gaine.

SONNET.
XIII.

IN that proud port, which her so goodly graceth,
    whiles her faire face she reares vp to the skie:
      and to the ground her eie lids low embaseth,
      most goodly temperature ye may descry,
Myld humblesse mixt with awfull maiesty.
    for looking on the earth whence she was borne,
      her minde remembreth her mortalitie,
      what so is fayrest shall to earth returne.

But that same lofty countenance seemes to scorne
  base thing, and thinke how she to heauen may clime:
  treading downe earth as lothsome and forlorne,
  that hinders heauenly thoughts with drossy slime.
Yet lowly still vouchsafe to looke on me,
  such lowlinesse shall make you lofty be.

REtourne agayne my forces late dismayd,
  Vnto the siege by you abandon'd quite,
  great shame it is to leaue like one afrayd,
  so fayre a peece for one repulse so light.
Gaynst such strong castles needeth greater might,
  then those small forts which ye were wont belay;
  such haughty mynds enur'd to hardy fight,
  disdayne to yield vnto the first assay.
Bring therefore all the forces that ye may,
  and lay incessant battery to her heart,
  playnts, prayers, vowes, ruth, sorrow, and dismay,
  those engins can the proudest loue conuert.
And if those fayle fall downe and dy before her,
  so dying liue, and liuing do adore her.

YE tradefull Merchants that with weary toyle,
  do seeke most pretious things to make your gain:
  and both the Indias of their treasures spoile,
  what needeth you to seeke so farre in vaine?
For loe my loue doth in her selfe containe
  all this worlds riches that may farre be found,
  if Saphyres, loe her eies be Saphyres plaine,
  if Rubies, loe hir lips be Rubies sound:
If Pearles, hir teeth be pearles both pure and round;
  if Yuorie, her forhead yuory weene;
  if Gold, her locks are finest gold on ground;
  if siluer, her faire hands are siluer sheene:
But that which fairest is, but few behold,
  her mind adornd with vertues manifold.

SONNET.
XVI.

ONe day as I vnwarily did gaze
  on those fayre eyes my loues immortall light:
  the whiles my stonisht hart stood in amaze,
  through sweet illusion of her lookes delight;
I mote perceiue how in her glauncing sight,
  legions of loues with little wings did fly:
  darting their deadly arrowes fyry bright,
  at euery rash beholder passing by.
One of those archers closely I did spy,
  ayming his arrow at my very hart:
  when suddenly with twincle of her eye,
  the Damzell broke his misintended dart.
Had she not so doon, sure I had bene slayne,
  yet as it was, I hardly scap't with paine.

SONNET.
XVII.

THe glorious pourtraict of that Angels face,
  Made to amaze weake mens confused skil:
  and this worlds worthlesse glory to embase,
  what pen, what pencill can expresse her fill?
For though he colours could deuize at will,
  and eke his learned hand at pleasure guide,
  least trembling it his workmanship should spill,
  yet many wondrous things there are beside.
The sweet eye-glaunces, that like arrowes glide,
  the charming smiles, that rob sence from the hart:
  the louely pleasance and the lofty pride,
  cannot expressed be by any art.
A greater craftesmans hand thereto doth neede,
  that can expresse the life of things indeed.

SONNET.
XVIII.

THe rolling wheele that runneth often round,
  The hardest steele in tract of time doth teare:
  and drizling drops that often doe redound,
  the firmest flint doth in continuance weare.
Yet cannot I with many a dropping teare,
  and long intreaty soften her hard hart:
  that she will once vouchsafe my plaint to heare,
  or looke with pitty on my payneful smart.

But when I pleade, she bids me play my part,
    and when I weep, she sayes teares are but water:
    and when I sigh, she sayes I know the art,
    and when I waile, she turnes hir selfe to laughter.
So doe I weepe, and wayle, and pleade in vaine,
    whiles she as steele and flint doth still remayne.

THe merry Cuckow, messenger of Spring,
    His trompet shrill hath thrise already sounded:
    that warnes al louers wayt vpon their king,
    who now is comming forth with girland crouned.
With noyse whereof the quyre of Byrds resounded
    their anthemes sweet devized of loues prayse,
    that all the woods theyr ecchoes back rebounded,
    as if they knew the meaning of their layes.
But mongst them all, which did Loues honor rayse
    no word was heard of her that most it ought,
    but she his precept proudly disobayes,
    and doth his ydle message set at nought.
Therefore O loue, vnlesse she turne to thee
    ere Cuckow end, let her a rebell be.

IN vaine I seeke and sew to her for grace,
    and doe myne humbled hart before her poure:
    the whiles her foot she in my necke doth place,
    and tread my life downe in the lowly floure.
And yet the Lyon that is Lord of power,
    and reigneth ouer euery beast in field:
    in his most pride disdeigneth to deuoure
    the silly lambe that to his might doth yield.
But she more cruell and more saluage wylde,
    then either Lyon or the Lyonesse:
    shames not to be with guiltlesse bloud defylde,
    but taketh glory in her cruelnesse.
Fayrer then fayrest let none euer say,
    that ye were blooded in a yeelded pray.

SONNET.
XXI.

WAs it the worke of nature or of Art,
    which tempred so the feature of her face,
    that pride and meeknesse mixt by equall part,
    doe both appeare t'adorne her beauties grace?
For with mild pleasance, which doth pride displace,
    she to her loue doth lookers eyes allure:
    and with sterne countenance back again doth chace
    their looser lookes that stir vp lustes impure.
With such strange termes her eyes she doth inure,
    that with one looke she doth my life dismay:
    and with another doth it streight recure,
    her smile me drawes, her frowne me driues away.
Thus doth she traine and teach me with her lookes,
    such art of eyes I neuer read in bookes.

SONNET.
XXII.

THis holy season fit to fast and pray,
    Men to deuotion ought to be inclynd:
    therefore, I lykewise on so holy day,
    for my sweet Saynt some seruice fit will find.
Her temple fayre is built within my mind,
    in which her glorious ymage placed is,
    on which my thoughts doo day and night attend
    lyke sacred priests that neuer thinke amisse.
There I to her as th'author of my blisse,
    will builde an altar to appease her yre:
    and on the same my hart will sacrifise,
    burning in flames of pure and chast desyre:
The which vouchsafe O goddesse to accept,
    amongst thy deerest relicks to be kept.

SONNET.
XXIII.

PEnelope for her Vlisses sake,
    Deuiz'd a Web her wooers to deceaue:
    in which the worke that she all day did make
    the same at night she did againe vnreaue:
Such subtile craft my Damzell doth conceaue,
    th'importune suit of my desire to shonne:
    for all that I in many dayes doo weaue,
    in one short houre I find by her vndonne.

So when I thinke to end that I begonne,
   I must begin and neuer bring to end:
   for with one looke she spils that long I sponne,
   and with one word my whole years work doth rend.
Such labour like the Spyders web I fynd,
   whose fruitlesse worke is broken with least wynd.

WHen I behold that beauties wonderment,
   And rare perfection of each goodly part:
   of natures skill the onely complement,
   I honor and admire the makers art.
But when I feele the bitter balefull smart,
   which her fayre eyes vnwares doe worke in mee:
   that death out of theyr shiny beames doe dart,
   I thinke that I a new *Pandora* see;
Whom all the Gods in councell did agree,
   into this sinfull world from heauen to send:
   that she to wicked men a scourge should bee,
   for all their faults with which they did offend.
But since ye are my scourge I will intreat,
   that for my faults ye will me gently beat.

SONNET.
XXIIII.

HOw long shall this lyke dying lyfe endure,
   And know no end of her owne mysery:
   but wast and weare away in termes vnsure,
   twixt feare and hope depending doubtfully?
Yet better were attonce to let me die,
   and shew the last ensample of your pride:
   then to torment me thus with cruelty,
   to proue your powre, which I too wel haue tride.
But yet if in your hardned brest ye hide
   a close intent at last to shew me grace:
   then all the woes and wrecks which I abide,
   as meanes of blisse I gladly wil embrace;
And wish that more and greater they might be,
   that greater meede at last may turne to mee.

SONNET.
XXV.

SONNET.
XXVI.

SWeet is the Rose, but growes vpon a brere;
    Sweet is the Iunipere, but sharpe his bough;
    sweet is the Eglantine; but pricketh nere;
    sweet is the firbloome, but his braunches rough.
Sweet is the Cypresse, but his rynd is tough,
    sweet is the nut, but bitter is his pill;
    sweet is the broome-flowre, but yet sowre enough;
    and sweet is Moly, but his root is ill.
So euery sweet with soure is tempred still,
    that maketh it be coueted the more:
    for easie things that may be got at will,
    most sorts of men doe set but little store.
Why then should I accoumpt of little paine,
    that endlesse pleasure shall vnto me gaine?

SONNET.
XXVII.

FAire proud now tell me why should faire be proud,
    Sith all worlds glorie is but drosse vncleane:
    and in the shade of death it selfe shall shroud,
    how euer now thereof ye little weene.
That goodly Idoll now so gay beseene,
    shall doffe her fleshes borowd fayre attyre:
    and be forgot as it had neuer beene,
    that many now much worship and admire.
Ne any then shall after it inquire,
    ne any mention shall thereof remaine:
    but what this verse, that neuer shall expyre,
    shall to you purchas with her thankles paine.
Faire be no lenger proud of that shall perish,
    but that which shal you make immortall, cherish.

SONNET.
XXVIII.

THe laurell leafe, which you this day doe weare,
    giues me great hope of your relenting mynd:
    for since it is the badg which I doe beare,
    ye bearing it doe seeme to me inclind:
The powre thereof, which ofte in me I find,
    let it lykewise your gentle brest inspire
    with sweet infusion, and put you in mind
    of that proud mayd, whom now those leaues attyre:

132

Proud *Daphne* scorning Phæbus louely fyre,
   on the Thessalian shore from him did flee:
   for which the gods in theyr reuengefull yre
   did her transforme into a laurell tree.
Then fly no more fayre loue from Phebus chace,
   but in your brest his leafe and loue embrace.

See how the stubborne damzell doth depraue
   my simple meaning with disdaynfull scorne:
   and by the bay which I vnto her gaue,
   accoumpts my selfe her captiue quite forlorne.
The bay (quoth she) is of the victours borne,
   yielded them by the vanquisht as theyr meeds,
   and they therewith doe poetes heads adorne,
   to sing the glory of their famous deedes.
But sith she will the conquest challeng needs,
   let her accept me as her faithfull thrall,
   that her great triumph which my skill exceeds,
   I may in trump of fame blaze ouer all.
Then would I decke her head with glorious bayes,
   and fill the world with her victorious prayse.

SONNET.
XXIX.

MY loue is lyke to yse, and I to fyre;
   how comes it then that this her cold so great
   is not dissolu'd through my so hot desyre,
   but harder growes the more I her intreat?
Or how comes it that my exceeding heat
   is not delayd by her hart frosen cold:
   but that I burne much more in boyling sweat,
   and feele my flames augmented manifold?
What more miracolous thing may be told
   that fire which all thing melts, should harden yse:
   and yse which is congeald with sencelesse cold,
   should kindle fyre by wonderfull deuyse?
Such is the powre of loue in gentle mind,
   that it can alter all the course of kynd.

SONNET.
XXX.

SONNET.
XXXI.

Ah why hath nature to so hard a hart,
    giuen so goodly giftes of beauties grace?
    whose pryde depraues each other better part,
    and all those pretious ornaments deface.
Sith to all other beastes of bloody race,
    a dreadfull countenaunce she giuen hath:
    that with theyr terrour al the rest may chace,
    and warne to shun the daunger of theyr wrath.
But my proud one doth worke the greater scath,
    through sweet allurement of her louely hew:
    that she the better may in bloody bath
    of such poore thralls her cruell hands embrew.
But did she know how ill these two accord,
    such cruelty she would haue soone abhord.

SONNET.
XXXII.

The paynefull smith with force of feruent heat,
    the hardest yron soone doth mollify:
    that with his heauy sledge he can it beat,
    and fashion to what he it list apply.
Yet cannot all these flames in which I fry,
    her hart more harde then yron soft awhit:
    ne all the playnts and prayers with which I
    doe beat on th'anduyle of her stubberne wit:
But still the more she feruent sees my fit,
    the more she frieseth in her wilfull pryde:
    and harder growes the harder she is smit,
    with all the playnts which to her be applyde.
What then remaines but I to ashes burne,
    and she to stones at length all frosen turne?

SONNET.
XXXIII.

GReat wrong I doe, I can it not deny,
    to that most sacred Empresse my dear dred,
    not finishing her Queene of faery,
    that mote enlarge her liuing prayses dead:
But lodwick, this of grace to me aread:
    doe ye not thinck th'accomplishment of it,
    sufficient worke for one mans simple head,
    all were it as the rest but rudely writ.

134

How then should I without another wit,
    thinck euer to endure so tædious toyle?
    sins that this one is tost with troublous fit,
    of a proud loue, that doth my spirite spoyle.
Ceasse then, till she vouchsafe to grawnt me rest,
    or lend you me another liuing brest.

Lyke as a ship that through the Ocean wyde,
    by conduct of some star doth make her way,
    whenas a storme hath dimd her trusty guyde,
    out of her course doth wander far astray.
So I whose star, that wont with her bright ray
    me to direct, with cloudes is ouercast,
    doe wander-now in darknesse and dismay,
    through hidden perils round about me plast.
Yet hope I well, that when this storme is past
    my *Helice* the lodestar of my lyfe
    will shine again, and looke on me at last,
    with louely light to cleare my cloudy grief.
Till then I wander carefull comfortlesse,
    in secret sorow and sad pensiuenesse.

MY hungry eyes through greedy couetize,
    still to behold the obiect of their paine:
    with no contentment can themselues suffize,
    but hauing pine and hauing not complaine.
For lacking it they cannot lyfe sustayne,
    and hauing it they gaze on it the more:
    in their amazement lyke *Narcissus* vaine
    whose eyes him staru'd: so plenty makes me poore.
Yet are mine eyes so filled with the store
    oft that faire sight, that nothing else they brooke,
    but lothe the things which they did like before,
    and can no more endure on them to looke.
All this worlds glory seemeth vayne to me,
    and all their showes but shadowes sauing she.

SONNET.
XXXVI.

TEll me when shall these wearie woes haue end,
    Or shall their ruthlesse torment neuer cease:
    but al my dayes in pining languor spend,
    without hope of aswagement or release?
Is there no meanes for me to purchace peace,
    or make agreement with her thrilling eyes:
    but that their cruelty doth still increace,
    and dayly more augment my miseryes?
But when ye haue shewed all extremityes,
    then thinke how litle glory ye haue gayned,
    by slaying him, whose lyfe though ye despyse,
    mote haue your life in honour long maintayned.
But by his death which some perhaps will mone,
    ye shall condemned be of many a one.

SONNET.
XXXVII.

WHat guyle is this, that those her golden tresses,
    She doth attyre vnder a net of gold:
    and with sly skill so cunningly them dresses,
    that which is gold or heare, may scarse be told?
Is it that mens frayle eyes, which gaze too bold,
    she may entangle in that golden snare:
    and being caught may craftily enfold
    theyr weaker harts, which are not wel aware?
Take heed therefore, myne eyes, how ye doe stare
    henceforth too rashly on that guilefull net,
    in which if euer ye entrapped are,
    out of her bands ye by no meanes shall get.
Fondnesse it were for any being free,
    to couet fetters, though they golden bee.

SONNET.
XXXVIII.

ARion, when through tempests cruel wracke,
    He forth was thrown into the greedy seas:
    through the sweet musick which his harp did make
    allur'd a Dolphin him from death to ease.
But my rude musick, which was wont to please
    some dainty eares, cannot with any skill,
    the dreadfull tempest of her wrath appease,
    nor moue the Dolphin from her stubborne will,

But in her pride she dooth perseuer still,
    all carelesse how my life for her decayse:
    yet with one word she can it saue or spill,
    to spill were pitty, but to saue were prayse.
Chose rather to be praysd for dooing good,
    then to be blam'd for spilling guiltlesse blood.

Sweet smile, the daughter of the Queene of loue,
    Expressing all thy mothers powrefull art:
    with which she wonts to temper angry loue,
    when all the gods he threats with thundring dart.
Sweet is thy vertue as thy selfe sweet art,
    for when on me thou shinedst late in sadnesse,
    a melting pleasance ran through euery part,
    and me reuiued with hart robbing gladnesse.
Whylest rapt with ioy resembling heauenly madnes,
    my soule was rauisht quite as in a traunce:
    and feeling thence no more her sorowes sadnesse,
    fed on the fulnesse of that chearefull glaunce.
More sweet than Nectar or Ambrosiall meat,
    seemd euery bit, which thenceforth I did eat.

MArk when she smiles with amiable cheare,
    And tell me whereto can ye lyken it:
    when on each eyelid sweetly doe appeare
    an hundred Graces as in shade to sit.
Lykest it seemeth in my simple wit
    vnto the fayre sunshine in somers day:
    that when a dreadfull storme away is flit,
    thrugh the broad world doth spred his goodly ray:
At sight whereof each bird that sits on spray,
    and euery beast that to his den was fled,
    comes forth afresh out of their late dismay,
    and to the light lift vp theyr drouping hed.
So my storme beaten hart likewise is cheared,
    with that sunshine when cloudy looks are cleared.

137

SONNET.
XLI.
Is it her nature or is it her will,
   to be so cruell to an humbled foe?
   if nature, then she may it mend with skill,
   if will, then she at will may will forgoe.
But if her nature and her wil be so,
   that she will plague the man that loues her most:
   and take delight t'encrease a wretches woe,
   then all her natures goodly guifts are lost.
And that same glorious beauties ydle boast,
   is but a bayt such wretches to beguile,
   as being long in her loues tempest tost,
   she meanes at last to make her piteous spoyle.
O fayrest fayre let neuer it be named,
   that so fayre beauty was so fowly shamed.

SONNET.
XLII.
THe loue which me so cruelly tormenteth,
   So pleasing is in my extreamest paine:
   that all the more my sorrow it augmenteth,
   the more I loue and doe embrace my bane.
Ne doe I wish (for wishing were but vaine)
   to be acquit fro my continuall smart:
   but ioy her thrall for euer to remayne,
   and yield for pledge my poore captyued hart;
The which that it from her may neuer start,
   let her, yf please her, bynd with adamant chayne:
   and from all wandring loues which mote peruart
   his safe assurance, strongly it restrayne.
Onely let her abstaine from cruelty,
   and doe me not before my time to dy.

SONNET.
XLIII.
SHall I then silent be or shall I speake?
   And if I speake, her wrath renew I shall:
   and if I silent be, my hart will breake,
   or choked be with ouerflowing gall.
What tyranny is this both my hart to thrall,
   and eke my toung with proud restraint to tie?
   that nether I may speake nor thinke at all,
   but like a stupid stock in silence die.

Yet I my hart with silence secretly
   will teach to speak, and my iust cause to plead:
   and eke mine eies with meeke humility,
   loue learned letters to her eyes to read.
Which her deep wit, that true harts thought can spel,
   wil soone conceiue, and learne to construe well.

WHen those renoumed noble Peres of Greece,
   thrugh stubborn pride amongst themselues did iar
   forgetfull of the famous golden fleece,
   then Orpheus with his harp theyr strife did bar.
But this continuall cruell ciuill warre,
   the which my selfe against my selfe doe make:
   whilest my weak powres of passions warreid arre,
   no skill can stint nor reason can aslake.
But when in hand my tunelesse harp I take,
   then doe I more augment my foes despight:
   and griefe renew, and passions doe awake
   to battaile fresh against my selfe to fight.
Mongst whome the more I seeke to settle peace,
   the more I fynd their malice to increace.

SONNET.
XLIIII.

LEaue lady in your glasse of christall clene,
   Your goodly selfe for euermore to vew:
   and in my selfe, my inward selfe I meane,
   most liuely lyke behold your semblant trew.
Within my hart, though hardly it can shew
   thing so diuine to vew of earthly eye:
   the fayre Idea of your celestiall hew,
   and euery part remaines immortally:
And were it not that through your cruelty,
   with sorrow dimmed and deformd it were:
   the goodly ymage of your visnomy,
   clearer then christall would therein appere.
But if your selfe in me ye playne will see,
   remoue the cause by which your fayre beames darkned be.

SONNET.
XLV.

SONNET.   WHen my abodes prefixed time is spent,
XLVI.
       My cruell fayre streight bids me wend my way:
       but then from heauen most hideous stormes are sent
       as willing me against her will to stay.
    Whom then shall I or heauen or her obay?
       the heauens know best what is the best for me:
       but as she will, whose will my life doth sway,
       my lower heauen, so it perforce must bee.
    But ye high heuens, that all this sorowe see,
       sith all your tempests cannot hold me backe:
       aswage your stormes, or else both you and she
       will both together me too sorely wrack.
    Enough it is for one man to sustaine
       the stormes, which she alone on me doth raine.

SONNET.   TRust not the treason of those smyling lookes,
XLVII.
       vntill ye haue theyr guylefull traynes well tryde:
       for they are lyke but vnto golden hookes,
       that from the foolish fish theyr bayts doe hyde:
    So she with flattring smyles weake harts doth guyde
       vnto her loue, and tempte to theyr decay,
       whome being caught she kills with cruell pryde,
       and feeds at pleasure on the wretched pray:
    Yet euen whylst her bloody hands them slay,
       her eyes looke louely and vpon them smyle:
       that they take pleasure in her cruell play,
       and dying doe them selues of payne beguyle.
    O mighty charm which makes men loue theyr bane,
       and thinck they dy with pleasure, liue with payne.

SONNET.   INnocent paper whom too cruell hand
XLVIII.
       Did make the matter to auenge her yre:
       and ere she could thy cause wel vnderstand,
       did sacrifize vnto the greedy fyre.
    Well worthy thou to haue found better hyre,
       then so bad end for hereticks ordayned:
       yet heresy nor treason didst conspire,
       but plead thy maisters cause vniustly payned.

140

Whom she all carelesse of his griefe constrayned
   to vtter forth the anguish of his hart:
   and would not heare, when he to her complayned
   the piteous passion of his dying smart.
Yet liue for euer, though against her will,
   and speake her good, though she requite it ill.

FAyre cruell, why are ye so fierce and cruell?
   Is it because your eyes haue powre to kill?
   then know, that mercy is the mighties iewell,
   and greater glory thinke to saue, then spill.
But if it be your pleasure and proud will,
   to shew the powre of your imperious eyes:
   then not on him that neuer thought you ill,
   but bend your force against your enemyes.
Let them feele th'utmost of your crueltyes,
   and kill with looks, as Cockatrices doo:
   but him that at your footstoole humbled lies,
   with mercifull regard, giue mercy too.
Such mercy shal you make admyred to be,
   so shall you liue by giuing life to me.

LOng languishing in double malady,
   of my harts wound and of my bodies griefe:
   there came to me a leach that would apply
   fit medicines for my bodies best reliefe.
Vayne man (quod I) that hast but little priefe,
   in deep discouery of the mynds disease,
   is not the hart of all the body chiefe?
   and rules the members as it selfe doth please?
Then with some cordialls seeke first to appease
   the inward languour of my wounded hart,
   and then my body shall haue shortly ease:
   but such sweet cordialls passe Physitions art.
Then my lyfes Leach doe you your skill reueale,
   and with one salue both hart and body heale.

SONNET.
LI.

DOe I not see that fayrest ymages
    Of hardest Marble are of purpose made?
    for that they should endure through many ages,
    ne let theyr famous moniments to fade.
Why then doe I, vntrainde in louers trade,
    her hardnes blame which I should more commend?
    sith neuer ought was excellent assayde,
    which was not hard t'atchiue and bring to end.
Ne ought so hard, but he that would attend,
    mote soften it and to his will allure:
    so doe I hope her stubborne hart to bend,
    and that it then more stedfast will endure.
Onely my paines wil be the more to get her,
    but hauing her, my ioy wil be the greater.

SONNET.
LII.

SO oft as homeward I from her depart,
    I goe lyke one that hauing lost the field,
    is prisoner led away with heauy hart,
    despoyld of warlike armes and knowen shield.
So doe I now my selfe a prisoner yeeld,
    to sorrow and to solitary paine:
    from presence of my dearest deare exylde,
    longwhile alone in languor to remaine.
There let no thought of ioy or pleasure vaine,
    dare to approch, that may my solace breed:
    but sudden dumps and drery sad disdayne
    of all worlds gladnesse more my torment feed.
So I her absens will my penaunce make,
    that of her presens I my meed may take.

SONNET.
LIII.

THe Panther knowing that his spotted hyde
    Doth please all beasts but that his looks them fray:
    within a bush his dreadfull head doth hide,
    to let them gaze whylest he on them may pray.
Right so my cruell fayre with me doth play:
    for with the goodly semblant of her hew,
    she doth allure me to mine owne decay,
    and then no mercy will vnto me shew.

Great shame it is, thing so diuine in view,
   made for to be the worlds most ornament:
   to make the bayte her gazers to embrew,
   good shames to be to ill an instrument.
But mercy doth with beautie best agree,
   as in theyr maker ye them best may see.

OF this worlds Theatre in which we stay,
   My loue lyke the Spectator ydly sits
   beholding me that all the pageants play,
   disguysing diuersly my troubled wits.
Sometimes I ioy when glad occasion fits,
   and mask in myrth lyke to a Comedy:
   soone after when my ioy to sorrow flits,
   I waile and make my woes a Tragedy.
Yet she beholding me with constant eye,
   delights not in my merth nor rues my smart:
   but when I laugh she mocks, and when I cry
   she laughes, and hardens euermore her hart.
What then can moue her? if nor merth nor mone,
   she is no woman, but a sencelesse stone.

SO oft as I her beauty doe behold,
   And therewith doe her cruelty compare:
   I maruaile of what substance was the mould
   the which her made attonce so cruell faire.
Not earth; for her high thoghts more heauenly are,
   not water; for her loue doth burne like fyre:
   not ayre; for she is not so light or rare,
   not fyre; for she doth friese with faint desire.
Then needs another Element inquire
   whereof she mote be made; that is the skye.
   for to the heauen her haughty lookes aspire:
   and eke her mind is pure immortall hye.
Then sith to heauen ye lykened are the best,
   be lyke in mercy as in all the rest.

143

SONNET.
LVI.

FAyre ye be sure, but cruell and vnkind,
   As is a Tygre that with greedinesse
   hunts after bloud, when he by chance doth find
   a feeble beast, doth felly him oppresse.
Fayre be ye sure, but proud and pittilesse,
   as is a storme, that all things doth prostrate:
   finding a tree alone all comfortlesse,
   beats on it strongly it to ruinate.
Fayre be ye sure, but hard and obstinate,
   as is a rocke amidst the raging floods:
   gaynst which a ship of succour desolate,
   doth suffer wreck both of her selfe and goods.
That ship, that tree, and that same beast am I,
   whom ye doe wreck, doe ruine, and destroy.

SONNET.
LVII.

SWeet warriour when shall I haue peace with you?
   High time it is, this warre now ended were:
   which I no lenger can endure to sue,
   ne your incessant battry more to beare:
So weake my powres, so sore my wounds appeare,
   that wonder is how I should liue a iot,
   seeing my hart through launched euery where
   with thousand arrowes, which your eies have shot:
Yet shoot ye sharpely still, and spare me not,
   but glory thinke to make these cruel stoures.
   ye cruell one, what glory can be got,
   in slaying him that would liue gladly yours?
Make peace therefore, and graunt me timely grace,
   that al my wounds wil heale in little space.

SONNET.
LVIII.

By her that is most assured to her selfe.

WEake is th'assurance that weake flesh reposeth
   In her owne powre, and scorneth others ayde:
   that soonest fals when as she most supposeth
   her selfe assurd, and is of nought affrayd.
All flesh is frayle, and all her strength vnstayd,
   like a vaine bubble blowen vp with ayre:

144

deuouring tyme and changeful chance haue prayd
    her glories pride that none may it repayre.
Ne none so rich or wise, so strong or fayre,
    but fayleth trusting on his owne assurance:
    and he that standeth on the hyghest stayre
    fals lowest: for on earth nought hath enduraunce.
Why then doe ye proud fayre, misdeeme so farre,
    that to your selfe ye most assured arre?

THrise happie she, that is so well assured
    Vnto her selfe and setled so in hart:
    that nether will for better be allured,
    ne feard with worse to any chaunce to start,
But like a steddy ship doth strongly part
    the raging waues and keepes her course aright:
    ne ought for tempest doth from it depart,
    ne ought for fayrer weathers false delight.
Such selfe assurance need not feare the spight
    of grudging foes, ne fauour seek of friends:
    but in the stay of her owne stedfast might,
    nether to one her selfe nor other bends.
Most happy she that most assured doth rest,
    but he most happy who such one loues best.

SONNET.
LIX.

THey that in course of heauenly spheares are skild,
    To euery planet point his sundry yeare:
    in which her circles voyage is fulfild,
    as Mars in three score yeares doth run his spheare.
So since the winged God his planet cleare,
    began in me to moue, one yeare is spent:
    the which doth longer vnto me appeare,
    then al those fourty which my life outwent.
Then by that count, which louers books inuent,
    the spheare of Cupid fourty yeares containes:
    which I haue wasted in long languishment,
    that seemd the longer for my greater paines.
But let my loues fayre Planet short her wayes
    this yeare ensuing, or else short my dayes.

SONNET.
LX.

SONNET.
LXI.

THe glorious image of the makers beautie,
   My souerayne saynt, the Idoll of my thought,
   dare not henceforth aboue the bounds of dewtie,
   t'accuse of pride, or rashly blame for ought.
For being as she is diuinely wrought,
   and of the brood of Angels heuenly borne:
   and with the crew of blessed Saynts vpbrought,
   each of which did her with theyr guifts adorne;
The bud of ioy, the blossome of the morne,
   the beame of light, whom mortal eyes admyre:
   what reason is it then but she should scorne
   base things that to her loue too bold aspire?
Such heauenly formes ought rather worshipt be,
   then dare be lou'd by men of meane degree.

SONNET.
LXII.

THe weary yeare his race now hauing run,
   The new begins his compast course anew:
   with shew of morning mylde he hath begun,
   betokening peace and plenty to ensew.
So let vs, which this chaunge of weather yew,
   chaunge eeke our mynds and former liues amend,
   the old yeares sinnes forepast let vs eschew,
   and fly the faults with which we did offend.
Then shall the new yeares ioy forth freshly send,
   into the glooming world his gladsome ray:
   and all these stormes which now his beauty blend,
   shall turne to caulmes and tymely cleare away.
So likewise loue cheare you your heauy spright,
   and chaunge old yeares annoy to new delight.

SONNET
LXIII.

AFter long stormes and tempests sad assay,
   Which hardly I endured heretofore:
   in dread of death and daungerous dismay,
   with which my silly barke was tossed sore:
I doe at length descry the happy shore,
   in which I hope ere long for to arryue:
   fayre soyle it seemes from far and fraught with store
   of all that deare and daynty is alyue.

Most happy he that can at last atchyue
    the ioyous safety of so sweet a rest:
    whose least delight sufficeth to depriue
    remembrance of all paines which him opprest.
All paines are nothing in respect of this,
    all sorrowes short that gaine eternall blisse.

COmming to kisse her lyps, (such grace I found)
    Me seemd I smelt a gardin of sweet flowres:
    that dainty odours from them threw around
    for damzels fit to decke their louers bowres.
Her lips did smell lyke vnto Gillyflowers,
    her ruddy cheekes lyke vnto Roses red:
    her snowy browes lyke budded Bellamoures,
    her louely eyes lyke Pincks but newly spred,
Her goodly bosome lyke a Strawberry bed,
    her neck lyke to a bounch of Cullambynes:
    her brest lyke lillyes, ere theyr leaues be shed,
    her nipples lyke yong blossomd Iessemynes:
Such fragrant flowres doe giue most odorous smell,
    but her sweet odour did them all excell.

THe doubt which ye misdeeme, fayre loue, is vaine,
    That fondly feare to loose your liberty,
    when loosing one, two liberties ye gayne,
    and make him bond that bondage earst dyd fly.
Sweet be the bands, the which true loue doth tye,
    without constraynt or dread of any ill:
    the gentle birde feeles no captiuity
    within her cage, but singes and feeds her fill.
There pride dare not approch, nor discord spill
    the league twixt them, that loyal loue hath bound:
    but simple truth and mutuall good will,
    seekes with sweet peace to salue each others wound:
There fayth doth fearlesse dwell in brasen towre,
    and spotlesse pleasure builds her sacred bowre.

SONNET.
LXVI.

TO all those happy blessings which ye haue,
   with plenteous hand by heauen vpon you thrown,
   this one disparagement they to you gaue,
   that ye your loue lent to se meane a one.
Yee whose high worths surpassing paragon,
   could not on earth haue found one fit for mate,
   ne but in heauen matchable to none,
   why did ye stoup vnto so lowly state?
But ye thereby much greater glory gate,
   then had ye sorted with a princes pere:
   for now your light doth more it selfe dilate,
   and in my darknesse greater doth appeare.
   Yet since your light hath once enlumind me,
   with my reflex yours shall encreased be.

SONNET.
LXVII.

Lyke as a huntsman after weary chace,
   Seeing the game from him escapt away,
   sits downe to rest him in some shady place,
   with panting hounds beguiled of their pray:
So after long pursuit and vaine assay,
   when I all weary had the chace forsooke,
   the gentle deare returnd the selfe-same way,
   thinking to quench her thirst at the next brooke
There she beholding me with mylder looke,
   sought not to fly, but fearelesse still did bide:
   till I in hand her yet halfe trembling tooke,
   and with her owne goodwill hir fyrmely tyde.
   Strange thing me seemd to see a beast so wyld,
   so goodly wonne with her owne will beguyld.

SONNET.
LXVIII.

MOst glorious Lord of lyfe that on this day,
   Didst make thy triumph ouer death and sin:
   and hauing harrowd hell didst bring away
   captiuity thence captiue vs to win:
This ioyous day, deare Lord, with ioy begin,
   and grant that we for whom thou diddest dye
   being with thy deare blood clene washt from sin,
   may liue for euer in felicity.

148

And that thy loue we weighing worthily,
    may likewise loue thee for the same againe:
    and for thy sake that all lyke deare didst buy,
    with loue may one another entertayne.
So let vs loue, deare loue, lyke as we ought,
    loue is the lesson which the Lord vs taught.

THe famous warriors of the anticke world,   SONNET.
    Vsed Trophees to erect in stately wize: LXIX.
    in which they would the records haue enrold,
    of theyr great deeds and valarous emprize.
What trophee then shall I most fit deuize,
    in which I may record the memory
    of my loues conquest, peerelesse beauties prise,
    adorn'd with honour, loue, and chastity.
Euen this verse vowd to eternity,
    shall be thereof immortall moniment:
    and tell her prayse to all posterity,
    that may admire such worlds rare wonderment.
The happy purchase of my glorious spoile,
    gotten at last with labour and long toyle.

FResh spring the herald of loues mighty king,   SONNET.
    In whose cote armour richly are displayd   LXX.
    all sorts of flowers the which on earth do spring
    in goodly colours gloriously arrayd:
Goe to my loue, where she is carelesse layd,
    yet in her winters bowre not well awake:
    tell her the ioyous time wil not be staid
    vnlesse she doe him by the forelock take.
Bid her therefore her selfe soone ready make,
    to wayt on loue amongst his louely crew:
    where euery one that misseth then her make,
    shall be by him amearst with penance dew.
Make hast therefore sweet loue, whilest it is prime,
    for none can call againe the passed time.

SONNET.
LXXI.

I Ioy to see how in your drawen work,
 Your selfe vnto the Bee ye doe compare;
 and me vnto the Spyder that doth lurke,
 in close awayt to catch her vnaware.
Right so your selfe were caught in cunning snare
 of a deare foe, and thralled to his loue:
 in whose streight bands ye now captiued are
 so firmely, that ye neuer may remoue.
But as your worke is wouen all aboue,
 with woodbynd flowers and fragrant Eglantine:
 so sweet your prison you in time shall proue,
 with many deare delights bedecked fyne.
And all thensforth eternall peace shall see,
 betweene the Spyder and the gentle Bee.

SONNET.
LXXII.

OFt when my spirit doth spred her bolder winges,
 In mind to mount vp to the purest sky:
 it down is weighd with thoght of earthly things
 and clogd with burden of mortality,
Where when that souerayne beauty it doth spy,
 resembling heauens glory in her light:
 drawne with sweet pleasures bayt, it back doth fly,
 and vnto heauen forgets her former flight.
There my fraile fancy fed with full delight,
 doth bath in blisse and mantleth most at ease:
 ne thinks of other heauen, but how it might
 her harts desire with most contentment please.
Hart need not wish none other happinesse,
 but here on earth to haue such heuens blisse.

SONNET.
LXXIII.

BEing my selfe captyued here in care,
 My hart, whom none with seruile bands can tye,
 but the fayre tresses of your golden hayre,
 breaking his prison forth to you doth fly.
Lyke as a byrd that in ones hand doth spy
 desired food, to it doth make his flight:
 euen so my hart, that wont on your fayre eye
 to feed his fill, flyes backe vnto your sight.

Doe you him take, and in your bosome bright,
    gently encage, that he may be your thrall:
    perhaps the there may learne with rare delight,
    to sing your name and prayses ouer all.
That it hereafter may you not repent,
    him lodging in your bosome to haue lent.

MOst happy letters fram'd by skilfull trade,
    with which that happy name was first desynd:
    the which three times thrise happy hath me made,
    with guifts of body, fortune and of mind.
The first my being to me gaue by kind,
    from mothers womb deriu'd by dew descent,
    the second is my souereigne Queene most kind,
    that honour and large richesse to me lent.
The third my loue, my liues last ornament,
    by whom my spirit out of dust was raysed:
    to speake her prayse and glory excellent,
    of all aliue most worthy to be praysed.
Ye three Elizabeths for euer liue,
    that three such graces did vnto me giue.

ONe day I wrote her name vpon the strand,
    but came the waues and washed it away:
    agayne I wrote it with a second hand,
    but came the tyde, and made my paynes his pray.
Vayne man, sayd she, that doest in vaine assay,
    a mortall thing so to immortalize,
    for I my selue shall lyke to this decay,
    and eek my name bee wyped out lykewize.
Not so, (quod I) let baser things deuize
    to dy in dust, but you shall liue by fame:
    my verse your vertues rare shall eternize,
    and in the heuens wryte your glorious name.
Where whenas death shall all the world subdew,
    our loue shall liue, and later life renew.

151

SONNET.
LXXVI.

FAyre bosome fraught with vertues richest tresure,
    The neast of loue, the lodging of delight:
    the bowre of blisse, the paradice of pleasure,
    the sacred harbour of that heuenly spright:
How was I rauisht with your louely sight,
    and my frayle thoughts too rashly led astray?
    whiles diuing deepe through amorous insight,
    on the sweet spoyle of beautie they did pray.
And twixt her paps like early fruit in May,
    whose haruest seemd to hasten now apace:
    they loosely did theyr wanton winges display,
    and there to rest themselues did boldly place.
Sweet thoughts I enuy your so happy rest,
    which oft I wisht, yet neuer was so blest.

SONNET.
LXXVII.

Was it a dreame, or did I see it playne,
    a goodly table of pure yvory:
    all spred with iuncats, fit to entertayne
    the greatest Prince with pompous roialty?
Mongst which there in a siluer dish did ly
    twoo golden apples of vnualewd price:
    far passing those which Hercules came by,
    or those which Atalanta did entice.
Exceeding sweet, yet voyd of sinfull vice,
    That many sought yet none could euer taste,
    sweet fruit of pleasure brought from paradice
    by Loue himselfe and in his garden plaste.
Her brest that table was so richly spredd,
    my thoughts the guests, which would thereon haue fedd.

SONNET.
LXXVIII.

Lackyng my loue I go from place to place,
    lyke a young fawne that late hath lost the hynd:
    and seeke each where, where last I sawe her face,
    whose ymage yet I carry fresh in mynd.
I seeke the fields with her late footing synd,
    I seeke her bowre with her late presence deckt,
    yet nor in field nor bowre I her can fynd:
    yet field and bowre are full of her aspect.

But when myne eyes I thereunto direct,
    they ydly back returne to me agayne,
    and when I hope to see theyr trew obiect,
    I fynd my selfe but fed with fancies vayne.
Ceasse then myne eyes, to seeke her selfe to see,
    and let my thoughts behold her selfe in mee.

MEn call you fayre, and you doe credit it, SONNET.
    For that your selfe ye dayly such doe see: LXXIX.
    but the trew fayre, that is the gentle wit,
    and vertuous mind, is much more praysd of me.
For all the rest, how euer fayre it be,
    shall turne to nought and loose that glorious hew:
    but onely that is permanent and free
    from frayle corruption, that doth flesh ensew.
That is true beautie: that doth argue you
    to be diuine and borne of heauenly seed:
    deriu'd from that fayre Spirit, from whom al true
    and perfect beauty did at first proceed.
He onely fayre, and what he fayre hath made,
    all other fayre lyke flowres vntymely fade.

AFter so long a race as I haue run SONNET.
    Through Faery land, which those six books compile, LXXX.
    giue leaue to rest me being halfe fordonne,
    and gather to my selfe new breath awhile.
Then as a steed refreshed after toyle,
    out of my prison I will breake anew:
    and stoutly will that second worke assoyle,
    with strong endeuour and attention dew.
Till then giue leaue to me in pleasant mew,
    to sport my muse and sing my loues sweet praise:
    the contemplation of whose heauenly hew,
    my spirit to an higher pitch will rayse.
But let her prayses yet be low and meane,
    fit for the handmayd of the Faery Queene.

SONNET.
LXXXI.

FAyre is my loue, when her fayre golden heares,
  with the loose wynd ye wauing chance to marke:
  fayre when the rose in her red cheekes appeares,
  or in her eyes the fyre of loue does sparke.
Fayre when her brest lyke a rich laden barke,
  with pretious merchandize she forth doth lay:
  fayre when that cloud of pryde, which oft doth dark
  her goodly light with smiles she driues away.
But fayrest she, when so she doth display
  the gate with pearles and rubyes richly dight:
  throgh which her words so wise do make their way
  to beare the message of her gentle spright.
The rest be works of natures wonderment,
  but this the worke of harts astonishment.

SONNET.
LXXXII.

IOy of my life, full oft for louing you
  I blesse my lot, that was so lucky placed:
  but then the more your owne mishap I rew,
  that are so much by so meane loue embased.
For had the equall heuens so much you graced
  in this as in the rest, ye mote inuent
  som heuenly wit, whose verse could haue enchased
  your glorious name in golden moniment.
But since ye deignd so goodly to relent
  to me your thrall, in whom is little worth,
  that little that I am, shall all be spent,
  in setting your immortall prayses forth.
Whose lofty argument vplifting me,
  shall lift you vp vnto an high degree.

SONNET.
LXXXIII.

MY hungry eyes, through greedy couetize,
  Still to behold the obiect of theyr payne:
  with no contentment can themselues suffize,
  but hauing pine, and hauing not complayne.
For lacking it, they cannot lyfe sustayne,
  and seeing it, they gaze on it the more:
  in theyr amazement lyke Narcissus vayne
  whose eyes him staru'd: so plenty makes me pore.

154

Yet are myne eyes so filled with the store
    of that fayre sight, that nothing else they brooke:
    but loath the things which they did like before,
    and can no more endure on them to looke.
All this worlds glory seemeth vayne to me,
    and all theyr shewes but shadowes sauing she.

LEt not one sparke of filthy lustfull fyre   SONNET.
    breake out, that may her sacred peace molest: LXXXIIII.
    ne one light glance of sensuall desyre
    Attempt to work her gentle mindes vnrest.
But pure affections bred in spotlesse brest,
    and modest thoughts breathd from wel tempred sprites,
    goe visit her in her chast bowre of rest,
    accompanyde with angelick delightes.
There fill your selfe with those most ioyous sights,
    the which my selfe could neuer yet attayne:
    but speake no word to her of these sad plights,
    which her too constant stiffenesse doth constrayn.
Onely behold her rare perfection,
    and blesse your fortunes fayre election.

THe world that cannot deeme of worthy things,   SONNET.
    when I doe praise her, say I doe but flatter: LXXXV.
    so does the Cuckow, when the Mauis sings,
    begin his witlesse note apace to clatter.
But they that skill not of so heauenly matter,
    all that they know not, enuy or admyre,
    rather then enuy let them wonder at her,
    but not to deeme of her desert aspyre.
Deepe in the closet of my parts entyre,
    her worth is written with a golden quill:
    that me with heauenly fury doth inspire,
    and my glad mouth with her sweet prayses fill.
Which when as fame in her shrill trump shal thunder,
    let the world chose to enuy or to wonder.

SONNET.
LXXXVI.

VEnemous toung tipt with vile adders sting,
    Of that selfe kynd with which the Furies fell
    theyr snaky heads doe combe, from which a spring
    of poysoned words and spitefull speeches well.
Let all the plagues and horrid paines of hell,
    vpon thee fall for thine accursed hyre:
    that with false forged lyes, which thou didst tel,
    in my true loue did stirre vp coles of yre,
The sparkes whereof let kindle thine own fyre,
    and catching hold on thine owne wicked hed
    consume thee quite, that didst with guile conspire
    in my sweet peace such breaches to haue bred.
Shame be thy meed, and mischiefe thy reward,
    dew to thy selfe that it for me prepard.

SONNET.
LXXXVII.

SInce I did leaue the presence of my loue,
    Many long weary dayes I haue outworne:
    and many nights, that slowly seemd to moue
    theyr sad protract from euening vntill morne.
For when as day the heauen doth adorne,
    I wish that night the noyous day would end:
    and when as night hath vs of light forlorne,
    I wish that day would shortly reascend.
Thus I the time with expectation spend,
    and faine my griefe with chaunges to beguile,
    that further seemes his terme still to extend,
    and maketh euery minute seeme a myle.
So sorrow still doth seeme too long to last,
    but ioyous houres doo fly away too fast.

SONNET.
LXXXVIII.

SInce I haue lackt the comfort of that light,
    The which was wont to lead my thoughts astray:
    I wander as in darknesse of the night,
    affrayd of euery dangers least dismay.
Ne ought I see, though in the clearest day,
    when others gaze vpon theyr shadowes vayne:
    but th'onely image of that heauenly ray,
    whereof some glance doth in mine eie remayne.

Of which beholding the Idæa playne,
    through contemplation of my purest part:
    with light thereof I doe my selfe sustayne,
    and thereon feed my loue-affamisht hart.
But with such brightnesse whylest I fill my mind,
    I starue my body and mine eyes doe blynd.

LYke as the Culuer on the bared bough,   SONNET.
    Sits mourning for the absence of her mate: LXXXIX.
    and in her songs sends many a wishfull vow,
    for his returne that seemes to linger late.
So I alone now left disconsolate,
    mourne to my selfe the absence of my loue:
    and wandring here and there all desolate,
    seek with my playnts to match that mournful doue:
Ne ioy of ought that vnder heauen doth houe,
    can comfort me, but her owne ioyous sight:
    whose sweet aspect both God and man can moue,
    in her vnspotted pleasauns to delight.
Dark is my day, whyles her fayre light I mis,
    and dead my life that wants such liuely blis.

TEXTUAL SOURCES

Sir Philip Sidney, *Astrophel and Stella,* a critical text based on the 1598 version, reprinted from W. A. Ringler, Jr., ed., *The Poems of Sir Philip Sidney* (Oxford: Oxford University Press, 1962).

Samuel Daniel, *Delia* (1592), reprinted from A. C. Sprague, ed., *Samuel Daniel: Poems and A Defence of Ryme* (Chicago: Chicago University Press, Phoenix Books, 1965).

Michael Drayton, *Ideas Mirrovr* (1594), reprinted from J. W. Hebel, ed., *The Works of Michael Drayton* (Oxford: Shakespeare Head Press, 1961), vol. I.

Edmund Spenser, *Amoretti* (1595) reprinted from E. Greenlaw et al., eds., *The Works of Edmund Spenser, A Variorum Edition,* vol. VIII: *The Minor Poems, Part Two,* ed. Ch. G. Osgood, H. G. Lotspeich (Baltimore: The Johns Jopkins Press, Fourth Printing, 1966).

BIBLIOGRAPHY

I. General Studies of the Sonnet Form and the English Sonnet

Ch. Tomlinson, *The Sonnet: Its Origin, Structure, and Place in Poetry* (London, 1874).

R. H. Stoddard, "The Sonnet in English Poetry", *Scribner's Monthly,* 22 (1881), 905-21.

J. A. Noble, *The Sonnet in England, and Other Essays* (London, 1893).

W. Sharp, "Sonnet: Its Characteristics and History", *Selected Writings of William Sharp,* vol. II: *Studies and Appreciations* (London, 1912), 1-70.

E. H. Wilkins, "The Invention of the Sonnet", *Modern Philology,* 13 (1915), 463-94.

W. H. Hulme, "The Most Popular English Verse and Stanzaic Forms", *Western Reserve Bulletin,* 23 (1920), 53 ff.

W. L. Bullock, "The Genesis of the English Sonnet Form", *PMLA,* 38 (1923), 729-44.

W. F. Schirmer, "Das Sonett in der englischen Literatur", *Anglia,* 49 (1925), 1-31.

T. W. H. Crosland, *The English Sonnet* (New York, 1917, repr. London, 1926).

W. C. Hall, "The Sonnet", *Manchester Quarterly,* 48 (1929), 262 ff.

E. Hamer, *The English Sonnet* (London, 1936).

W. Brewer, *Sonnets and Sestinas* (Boston, 1937).

A. Michelagnoli, *Il sonetto nella letteratura inglese* (Padua, 1938).

O. Kleinschmidt, "Die Kunst des Sonettes: Regel und Rhythmus im Gedicht", *Zeitschrift für Deutschkunde,* 53 (1939), 241-6.

C. D. Morley, "Sonnet", *Letters of Askance* (Philadelphia, 1939).

T. D. Ordeman, "How Many Rhyme Schemes has the Sonnet? " *College English,* 1 (1939), 171-3.

H. Timrod, "Character and Scope of the Sonnet", *Essays of Henry Timrod* (Univ. of Georgia Pr., 1942).

W. Mönch, *Das Sonett: Gestalt und Geschichte* (Heidelberg, 1955).

H. Palmer, "The English Sonnet", *Poetry Review,* 48 (1957), 215-8; 49 (1958), 26-8 and 84-7.

R. M. Burgess, "The Sonnet – a Cosmopolitan Literary Form – in the Renaissance", *Actes du IVᵉ Congrès de l'Association Internationale de Littérature Comparée, Fribourg, 1964,* ed. F. Jost (The Hague, 1966), 169-84.

P. Cruttwell, *The English Sonnet,* Writers and Their Work, 191 (London, 1966).

II. The Elizabethan Sonnet

K. Lentzner, *Über das Sonett und seine Gestaltung in der englischen Dichtung bis Milton,* Diss. (Halle, 1886).

G. Saintsbury, *A History of Elizabethan Literature* (London, 1887).

E. Koeppel, "Studien zur Geschichte des englischen Petrarkismus im sechzehnten Jahrhundert", *Romanische Forschungen,* 5 (1890), 65-98.

J. Erskine, *The Elizabethan Lyric* (Columbia Univ., 1903).

J. S. Harrison, *Platonism in English Poetry of the Sixteenth and Seventeenth Centuries* (New York, 1903).

D. E. Owen, *Relations of the Elizabethan Sonnet Sequences to Earlier English Verse* (1903).

S. Lee, ed., *Elizabethan Sonnets* (London, 1904, repr. New York, 1964), cf. introduction, vol. I, ix-cx.

P. E. More, "Elizabethan Sonnets", *Shelburn Essays,* Second Series (New York, 1905), 1-19.

I. Zocco, *Petrarchismo e Petrarchisti in Inghilterra* (Palermo, 1906).

P. H. Frye, "The Elizabethan Sonnet", *Literary Reviews and Criticisms* (London, 1908).

S. Lee, "The Elizabethan Sonnet", *Cambridge History of English Literature,* ed. A. W. Ward and A. R. Waller, vol. III (Cambridge, 1909), 247-88.

W. J. Courthope, *A History of English Poetry,* cf. vol. II (London, 1904), vol. III (London, 1911).

E. Kaun, *Konventionelles in den elisabethanischen Sonetten,* Diss. (Greifswald, 1915).

R. M. Alden, "The Lyrical Conceit of the Elizabethans", *Studies in Philology,* 14 (1917), 130-53.

A. Cruse, *The Elizabethan Lyrists and Their Poetry* (London, 1919).

J. G. Scott. "Minor Elizabethan Sonneteers and Their Greater Predecessors", *Review of English Studies,* 2 (1926), 423-7.

J. G. Scott, "The Names of the Heroines of Elizabethan Sonnet Sequences", *Review of English Studies,* 2 (1926), 159-62.

D. Bray, "The Art Form of the Elizabethan Sonnet Sequence and Shakespeare's Sonnets", *Shakespeare Jahrbuch,* 63 (1927), 159-82.

H. K. Hasselkuss, *Der Petrarkismus in der Sprache der Sonettdichter der Renaissance* (Münster, 1927).

J. G. Scott, *Les sonnets élisabéthains: les sources et l'apport personnel* (Paris, 1929).

L. B. Salomon, *The Devil Take Her* (Univ. of Pennsylvania, 1931).

L. E. Pearson, *Elizabethan Love Conventions* (Univ. of California, 1933, repr. London, 1966).

L. C. John, *The Elizabethan Sonnet Sequences: Studies in Conventional Conceits,* Columbia University Studies in English and Comparative Literature, 133 (New York, 1936, repr. 1964).

Y. Winters, "The 16th Century Lyric in England", *Poetry,* 53 (1939), 258-72 and 320-5, 54 (1939), 35-51, repr. *Elizabethan Poetry: Modern Essays in Criticism,* ed. P. J. Alpers (New York, 1967), 93-125.

Ch. F. Kremer, Jr., "Studies in Verse Form in Non-dramatic English Poetry from Wyatt to Sidney", *North Western University Summaries of Doctoral Dissertations,* 10 (1942), 30-2.

P. N. Siegel, "The Petrarchan Sonneteers and Neo-Platonic Love", *Studies in Philology,* 42 (1945), 164-82.

N. C. Stageberg, "The Aesthetic of the Petrarchan Sonnet", *Journal of Aesthetics and Art Criticism,* 7 (1948), 132-7.

A. B. Miller, "Themes and Techniques in Mid-Tudor Lyric Poetry: An Analytical Study of the Short Poems from Wyatt to Sidney", *Northwestern University Summaries of Doctoral Dissertations,* 17 (1950), 35-41.

C. Ing, *Elizabethan Lyrics* (London, 1951).

H. Smith, *Elizabethan Poetry: A Study in Conventions, Meanings, and Expressions* (Cambridge, Mass., 1952).

C. S. Lewis, *English Literature in the Sixteenth Century Excluding Drama,* Oxford History of English Literature, vol. III (Oxford, 1954).

J. L. Potter, "The Development of Sonnet Patterns in the Sixteenth Century", Diss. Harvard, 1954, *Doct. Diss. Accepted by American Universities* (1953-4), No. 21.

M. Evans, *English Poetry in the Sixteenth Century* (London, 1955).

C. Falls, "Penelope Rich and the Poets: Philip Sidney to John Ford", *Essays by Divers Hands,* 28 (1955), 123-37.

A. L. Sells, *The Italian Influence in English Poetry* (Bloomington, Ind., 1955).

J. W. Lever, *The Elizabethan Love Sonnet* (London, 1956).

J. Espiner-Scott, "Les sonnets élisabethains: Cupidon et l'influence d'Ovide", *Revue de Littérature comparée,* 31 (1957), 421-6.

Ch. Nelson, *Renaissance Theory of Love* (New York, 1958).

M. Valency, *In Praise of Love:* An Introduction to the Love Poetry of the Renaissance (New York, 1958).

F. T. Prince, "The Sonnet from Wyatt to Shakespeare", *Elizabethan Poetry,* ed. J. R. Brown and B. Harris, Stratford-upon-Avon Studies, 2 (London, 1960).

161

S. Baldi, "Il petrarchismo e la lirica elisabetiana", *Cultura e scuola,* 1 (1961), 56-64.

J. B. Leishman, *Themes and Variations in Shakespeare's Sonnets* (London, 1961).

C. Schaar, *On the Motif of Death in 16th Century English Sonnet Poetry,* Scripta minora Regiae Societatis humaniorum litterarum Ludensis, 1959-60 (Lund, 1961).

L. N. Goldman, "Attitudes Toward the Mistress in Five Elizabethan Sonnet Sequences", Diss. Univ. of Illinois, 1964, *Dissertation Abstracts,* 25 (1965), 6590-1.

H. M. Richmond, *The School of Love: The Evolution of the Stuart Love Lyric* (Princeton, 1964).

J. L. Hineley, "The Sonnet Sequence in Elizabethan Poetry", *Dissertation Abstracts,* 27 (1967), 3011 A.

D. L. Peterson, *The English Lyric from Wyatt to Donne: A History of the Plain and Eloquent Styles* (Princeton, N. J., 1966).

III. Sir Philip Sidney, *Astrophel and Stella*

Ch. Lamb, "Some Sonnets of Sir Philip Sidney", Last Essays of Elia, *Prose Works* (London, 1838), vol. III, 138-52.

E. Koeppel, "Sidneiana", *Anglia,* 10 (1888), 522-32.

A. W. Pollard, ed., *Astrophel and Stella* (London, 1888), cf. notes.

E. Koeppel, "Zu 'Astrophel and Stella'", *Anglia,* 13 (1891), 467-8.

K. Helm, "Zur Entstehung von Philip Sidneys Sonetten", *Anglia,* 19 (1897), 549-53.

S. Lee, ed., *Elizabethan Sonnets* (London, 1904, repr. New York, 1964), cf. introduction, vol. I, xxxii-xlix.

J. B. Fletcher, "Did 'Astrophel' love 'Stella'? ",*Modern Philology,* 5 (1907), 253-64.

S. P. Sherman, "Stella and 'The Broken Heart'", *PMLA,* 24 (1909), 274-85.

R. G. Wigham, O. F. Emerson, "Sonnet Structure in Sidney's 'Astrophel and Stella'", *Studies in Philology,* 18 (1921), 347-52.

J. G. Scott, "Parallels to Three Elizabethan Sonnets", *Modern Language Review,* 21 (1926), 190-2.

J. M. Purcell, "A Cup for my Lady Penelope", *Modern Language Notes,* 45 (1930), 310.

J. M. Purcell, "Sonnet CV of 'Astrophel and Stella' and 'Love's Labour's Lost' (IV, ii, 26-41)", *Philological Quarterly,* 10 (1931), 399.

M. Wilson, ed. *Astrophel and Stella* (London, 1931), cf. introduction and notes.

M. Wilson, *Sir Philip Sidney* (London, 1931).

J. M. Purcell, "A Note on Sonnet II of 'Astrophel and Stella'", *Philological Quarterly*, 11 (1932), 402-3.

L. C. John, "The Date of the Marriage of Penelope Devereux", *PMLA*, 49 (1934), 961-2.

J. M. Purcell, *Sidney's Stella* (Oxford, 1934).

T. H. Banks, "Sidney's 'Astrophel and Stella' Reconsidered", *PMLA*, 50 (1935), 403-12.

H. Hudson, "Penelope Devereux as Sidney's Stella", *Huntington Library Bulletin*, 7 (1935), 89-129.

K. O. Myrick, *Sir Philip Sidney as a Literary Craftsman* (Cambridge, Mass., 1935, repr. Lincoln, Nebraska, 1965).

J. M. Purcell, "Sidney's 'Astrophel and Stella' and Greville's 'Caelica'", *PMLA*, 50 (1935), 413-22.

W. G. Friedrich, "The Stella of Astrophel", *ELH*, 3 (1936), 114-39.

L. C. John, *The Elizabethan Sonnet Sequences: Studies in Conventional Conceits*, Columbia University Studies in English and Comparative Literature, 133 (New York, 1936, repr. 1964), cf. appendix.

J. H. Walter, "'Astrophel and Stella' and the 'Romaunt of the Rose'", *Review of English Studies*, 15 (1939), 265-73.

T. Spencer, "The Poetry of Sir Philip Sidney", *ELH*, 12 (1945), 251-78.

E. C. Pettet, "Sidney and the Cult of Romantic Love", *English*, 6 (1946-7), 232-40.

A. Thaler, *Shakespeare and Sir Philip Sidney* (Cambridge, Mass., 1947).

M. Poirier, *Sir Philip Sidney* (Lille, 1948).

J. M. Bullitt, "The Use of Rhyme Link in the Sonnets of Sidney, Drayton, and Spenser", *Journal of English and Germanic Philology*, 49 (1950), 14-32.

K. M. Murphy, "The 109th and 110th Sonnets of 'Astrophel and Stella'", *Philological Quarterly*, 34 (1955), 349-52.

R. L. Montgomery, Jr., "Reason, Passion, and Introspection in 'Astrophel and Stella'", *University of Texas Studies in English*, 36 (1957), 127-40.

M. Poirier, ed. and transl., *Astrophel et Stella* (Paris, 1957).

R. B. Young, *Three Studies in the Renaissance: Sidney, Jonson, Milton* (New Haven, 1958).

C. S. Burhans, "Sidney's 'With How Sad Steps, O Moon'", *The Explicator*, 18 (1959-60), 4, 26.

J. Buxton, "On the Date of 'Syr P. S. His Astrophel and Stella', . . . Printed for Matthew Lownes", *Bodleian Library Record*, 6 (1960), 614-6.

K. Muir, "'Astrophel and Stella', XXXI", *Notes & Queries*, 7 (1960), 51-2.

K. Muir, *Sir Philip Sidney*, Writers and Their Work, 120 (London, 1960).

J. Robertson, "Sir Philip Sidney and His Poetry", *Elizabethan Poetry*, ed.

J. R. Brown and B. Harris, Stratford-upon-Avon Studies, 2 (London, 1960), 111-30.

J. Stillinger, "The Biographical Problem of 'Astrophel and Stella'", *Journal of English and Germanic Philology*, 59 (1960), 617-39.

M. Putzel, "'Astrophel and Stella', XIV", *The Explicator*, 19 (1960-1), 4, 25.

R. L. Montgomery, Jr., *Symmetry and Sense: The Poetry of Sir Philip Sidney* (Austin, Texas, 1961).

C. R. B. Combellack, "Sidney's 'With How Sad Steps, O Moon'", *The Explicator*, 20 (1961-2), 3, 25.

S. A. Cowan, F. A. Dudley, "Sidney's 'Astrophel and Stella', IX, 12-14", *The Explicator*, 20 (1961-2), 9, 76.

E. H. Essig, "Sidney's 'With How Sad Steps, O Moon'", *The Explicator*, 20 (1961-2), 3, 25.

J. P. Castley, S. J., "'Astrophel and Stella' – 'High Sidnaean Love' or Courtly Compliment? ", *Melbourne Critical Review*, 5 (1962), 54-65.

W. A. Ringler, ed., *The Poems of Sir Philip Sidney* (Oxford, 1962), cf. commentary, 435-91.

A. R. Howe, "A Critical Edition of Sir Philip Sidney's 'Astrophel and Stella', with an Introduction", *Dissertation Abstracts*, 23 (1963), 1686.

V. Gentili, "La 'Tragicomedy' dell' 'Astrophil and Stella'", *Annali dell' Università di Lecce* (Facoltà di Lettere e Filosofia e di Magistero), 1 (1963-4), 57-92.

J. F. Cotter, "A Glasse of Reason: The Art of Poetry in Sidney's 'Astrophil and Stella'", Diss. Fordham Univ., 1963, *Dissertation Abstracts*, 24 (1964), 5382.

A. R. Howe, "Astrophel and Stella: 'Why and How'", *Studies in Philology*, 61 (1964), 150-69.

J. F. Mahoney, "The Philosophical Coherence and Literary Motive of 'Astrophel and Stella'", *Essays and Studies in Language and Literature*, ed. H. H. Petit (Pittsburgh, Pa., 1964).

V. Gentili, ed., *Astrophil and Stella* (Bari, 1965), cf. introduction and commentary.

D. Kalstone, *Sidney's Poetry: Contexts and Interpretations* (Cambridge, Mass., 1965). The chapter on 'Astrophel and Stella' is repr. in *Elizabethan Poetry: Modern Essays in Criticism*, ed. P. J. Alpers (New York, 1967).

E. G. Fogel, "The Mythical Sorrows of Astrophil", *Studies in Language and Literature in Honour of Margaret Schlauch*, ed. M. Brahmer, S. Helsztyński, J. Kryźanowski (Warsaw, 1966), 133-52.

F. Marenko, "Astrophil and Stella (I)", *Filologia e letteratura*, 13 (1967), 72-91.

N. Rudenstein, *Sidney's Poetic Development* (Cambridge, Mass., 1967).

S. M. Cooper, Jr., *The Sonnets of 'Astrophel and Stella': A Stylistic Study,* Studies in English Literature, 41 (The Hague, 1968).

IV. Samuel Daniel, *Delia*

"Samuel Daniel's Poems", anon., *Retrospective Review,* 8 (1823), 227-46.

H. Isaac, "Wie weit geht die Abhängigkeit Shakespeares von Samuel Daniel? Eine Studie zur Renaissancelyrik", *Shakespeare Jahrbuch,* 17 (1882), 165-200.

J. Guggenheim, *Quellenstudien zu Samuel Daniels Sonettenzyklus 'Delia',* Diss. (Berlin, 1898).

E. Spencer, *Alliteration in Spenser's Poetry . . . Compared with . . . Michael Drayton and Samuel Daniel,* Diss. (Zürich, 1898).

H. C. Beeching, "Delia", *Notes & Queries,* 100 (Aug. 26, 1899), 170-1.

A. E. Thiselton, "A Note on 'Delia' ", *Notes & Queries,* 100 (Oct. 7, 1899), 293.

S. Lee, ed., *Elizabethan Sonnets* (London, 1904, repr. New York, 1964), cf. introduction, vol. I, xlix-lxi.

W. W. Greg, *Pastoral Poetry and Pastoral Drama* (London, 1906).

L. E. Kastner, "The Elizabethan Sonneteers and the French Poets", *Modern Language Review,* 3 (1907), 268-277.

C. Ruutz-Rees, "Some Debts of Samuel Daniel to Du Bellay", *Modern Language Notes,* 24 (1909), 134-137.

G. R. Redgrave, "Daniel and the Emblem Literature", *Transactions of the Bibliographical Society,* 11 (1909-11), 39-58.

L. E. Kastner, "The Italian Sources of Daniel's 'Delia'", *Modern Language Review,* 7 (1912), 153-156.

R. M. Alden, *The Sonnets of Shakespeare* (New York, 1916).

G. K. Brady, *Samuel Daniel: A Critical Study* (Urbana, Illinois, 1923).

"Samuel Daniel, an Elizabethan Wordsworth", *Dublin Review,* 176 (1925), 108-17.

J. M. Robertson, *The Problems of the Shakespeare Sonnets* (London, 1926).

H. E. Rollins, ed., *The Sonnets, by Shakespeare,* New Variorum Edition (Philadelphia, 1944), cf. vol. II, 117-9.

J. Buxton, *Sir Philip Sidney and the English Renaissance* (London, 1954).

E. H. Miller, "Samuel Daniel's Revisions in 'Delia' ", *Journal of English and Germanic Philology,* 53 (1954), 58-68.

C. Schaar, "A Textual Puzzle in Daniel's 'Delia' ", *English Studies,* 40 (1954), 382-385.

C. C. Seronsky, "Well-languaged Daniel: a Reconsideration", *Modern Language Review,* 52 (1957), 481-497.

C. Schaar, *An Elizabethan Sonnet Problem: Shakespeare's Sonnets, Daniel's 'Delia' and Their Literary Background,* Lund Studies in English, 28 (Copenhagen, 1960).

P. Ure, "Two Elizabethan Poets: Samuel Daniel and Sir Walter Ralegh", *A Guide to English Literature,* ed. B. Ford, vol. II: *The Age of Shakespeare* (London, 1961), 123-38.

R. G. Adamany, "Daniel's Debt to Foreign Literatures and 'Delia' Edited", Diss. University of Wisconsin, 1963, *Dissertation Abstracts,* 23 (1963), 4350-1.

J. Rees, *Samuel Daniel: A Critical and Biographical Study,* Liverpool English Texts and Studies, 9 (Liverpool, 1964).

M. M. Johnson, "The Well-rimed Daniel: An Examination of 'Delia' and 'A Defence of Rhyme'", Diss. University of Arkansas, 1965, *Dissertation Abstracts,* 26 (1966), 4661.

P. Thomson, "Sonnet 15 of Samuel Daniel's 'Delia': A Petrarchan Imitation", *Comparative Literature,* 17 (1965), 151-7.

C. Seronsky, *Samuel Daniel,* Twayne's English Authors Series, 49 (New York, 1967).

L. Goldman, "Samuel Daniel's 'Delia' and the Emblem Tradition", *Journal of English and Germanic Philology,* 67 (1968), 49-63.

P. Spriet, *Samuel Daniel (1563-1619), sa vie, son œuvre,* thèse (Paris, 1968).

C. F. Williamson, "The Design of Daniel's 'Delia' ", *Review of English Studies,* 19 (1968), 251-260.

V. Michael Drayton, *Ideas Mirrovr*

J. P. Collier, "Michael Drayton and his 'Idea's Mirror'", *Gentleman's Magazine,* 34 (Sept., 1850), 262-5.

J. P. Collier, "Idea's Mirror", *Notes & Queries,* 26 (Nov. 29, 1862), 422.

O. Elton, *An Introduction to Michael Drayton* (Manchester, 1895).

E. Spencer, *Alliteration in Spenser's Poetry . . . Compared with . . . Michael Drayton and Samuel Daniel,* Diss. (Zürich, 1898).

H. C. Beeching, "The Sonnets of Michael Drayton", *Literature,* 5 (Aug. 19, 1899), 181-3.

W. J. Courthope, *A History of English Poetry* (London, 1903), cf. vol. III, chap. III.

H. C. Beeching, "A Note on the Sonnets of Michael Drayton in their Relation to Shakespeare's", *The Sonnets of Shakespeare* (Boston, 1904), 132-9.

S. Lee, ed., *Elizabethan Sonnets* (London, 1904, repr. New York, 1964), cf. introduction, vol. I, Lxxxv-xci.

L. Whitaker, "Michael Drayton as a Dramatist", *Modern Philology,* 1 (1904), 563-7.

O. Elton, *Michael Drayton: A Critical Study* (London, 1905, repr. New York, 1966).

C. Brett, ed., *Minor Poems of Michael Drayton* (Oxford, 1907), cf. introduction.

R. M. Alden, *The Sonnets of Shakespeare* (New York, 1916).

R. Hillyer, "The Drayton Sonnets", *The Freeman,* 6 (Jan. 31, 1923), 488-489.

J. W. Hebel, "Drayton and Shakespeare", *Modern Language Notes,* 40 (1926), 248-50.

B. Newdigate, "Michael Drayton and his 'Idea' ", *Dublin Review,* 200 (Jan., 1937), 79-92.

F. Y. St. Clair, "Drayton's First Revision of his Sonnets", *Studies in Philology,* 36 (1939), 40-59.

J. Robertson, "Drayton and the Countess of Pembroke", *Review of English Studies,* 16 (1940), 49.

M. Praz, "Michael Drayton", *English Studies,* 28 (1947), 97-101.

J. M. Bullitt, "The Use of Rhyme Link in the Sonnets of Sidney, Drayton, and Spenser", *Journal of English and Germanic Philology,* 49 (1950), 14-32.

J. Buxton, ed., *Poems of Michael Drayton* (Cambridge, Mass., 1953), cf. vol. I, preface.

J. W. Hebel, ed., *The Works of Michael Drayton* (Oxford, 1961), cf. vol. V: *Introduction, Notes, Variant Readings,* ed. K. Tillotson and B. H. Newdigate, 13-19.

L. Perrine, "A Drayton Sonnet", *CEA Critic,* 25 (1963), 8.

J. S. Philipson, "A Drayton Sonnet", *CEA Critic,* 25 (1963), 3.

P. G. Buchloh, *Michael Drayton: Barde und Historiker, Politiker und Prophet,* Kieler Beiträge zur Anglistik und Amerikanistik, 1 (Neumünster, 1964).

J. A. Berthelot, *Michael Drayton,* Twayne's English Authors Series, 52 (New York, 1967).

J. Buxton, *A Tradition of Poetry* (London, 1967).

R. F. Hardin, "Michael Drayton and the Ovidian Tradition", *Dissertation Abstracts,* 27 (1967), 3428 A.

J. Schönert, "Draytons Sonett-Revisionen", *Anglia,* 85 (1967), 161-83.

VI. Edmund Spenser, *Amoretti*

G. Chalmers, *Supplemental Apology* (London, 1799), 21-39.

"An Elizabethan Courtship", *Penn. Monthly,* 6 (1875), 739-48.

F. T. Palgrave, "Essays on the Minor Poems of Spenser, VII: Amoretti", *The Complete Works in Verse and Prose of Edmund Spenser,* ed. A. B. Grosart (London, 1882), vol. IV, lxxxvii-xcii.

S. F. Sears, *The Sources of Spenser's 'Amoretti',* M. A. Thesis (Columbia University, 1898).

E. Spencer, *Alliteration in Spenser's Poetry . . . Compared with . . . Michael Drayton and Samuel Daniel,* Diss. (Zürich, 1898).

J. B. Fletcher, "Mr. Sidney Lee and Spenser's 'Amoretti'", *Modern Language Notes,* 18 (1903), 111-3.

S. Lee, ed., *Elizabethan Sonnets* (London, 1904, repr. New York, 1964), cf. introduction, vol. I, xcii-xcix.

J. F. Kelly, "Note on Three Sonnets", *Revue Hispanique,* 13 (1905), 257-60.

P. W. Long, "Spenser and Lady Carey", *Modern Language Review,* 3 (1907), 257-67.

L. E. Kastner, "Spenser's 'Amoretti' and Desportes", *Modern Language Review,* 4 (1908), 65-69.

J. C. Smith, "The Problem of Spenser's Sonnets", *Modern Language Review,* 5 (1910), 273-281.

H. Littledale, "A Note on Spenser's 'Amoretti' ", *Modern Language Review,* 6 (1911), 203.

P. W. Long, "Spenser's Sonnets 'As Published' ", *Modern Language Review,* 6 (1911), 390-7.

E. J. Macintire, "French Influence on English Classicism", *PMLA,* 26 (1911), 496-527.

J. C. Smith, E. De Selincourt, *The Poetical Works of Edmund Spenser* (London, 1912), cf. introduction, xxxv ff.

E. G. Harman, *Edmund Spenser and the Impersonation of Francis Bacon* (London, 1914), cf. chap. IV.

F. J. Carpenter, *A Reference Guide to Edmund Spenser* (Chicago, 1923), cf. 175-9.

H. W. Garrod, "Spenser and Elizabeth Boyle", *Times Literary Supplement,* 22 (May 10 and 24, 1923), 321, 355.

M. Y. Hughes, "Spenser and the Greek Pastoral Triad", *Studies in Philology,* 20 (1923), 184-215.

F. I. Carpenter, "G. W. Senior and G. W. I.", *Modern Philology,* 22 (1924), 67-8.

W. L. Renwick, *Edmund Spenser* (London, 1925).

E. Legouis, *Edmund Spenser* (New York, 1926).

J. G. Scott, "The Sources of Spenser's 'Amoretti' ", *Modern Language Review,* 22 (1927), 189-95.

D. Hamer, "Spenser's First Marriage", Review *of English Studies,* 7 (1931), 271-90.

W. H. Welply, "Edmund Spenser: Being an Account of Some Recent Researches into His Life and Lineage, With some Notice of His Family and Descendants", *Notes & Queries,* ser. xiv, 6 (1932), 182-7.

H. M. Priest, "Tasso in English Literature 1575-1675", Summaries of Ph. D. Dissertations, Northwestern University, 1 (1933), 5-9.

I. Baroway, "The Imagery of Spenser and the Song of Songs", *Journal of English and Germanic Philology,* 33 (1934), 23-45.

F. Dannenberg, "Shakespeare's Sonette: Herkunft, Wesen, Deutung", *Shakespeare Jahrbuch,* 70 (1934), 37-64, cf. 41-2.

M. M. Hartmann, "Spenser's Conceits", Diss. University of Virginia, *Doctoral Diss. Accepted by American Universities* (1936-7), No. 4.

J. A. S. McPeek, *Catullus in Strange and Distant Britain,* Harvard Studies in Comparative Literature, 15 (Cambridge, Mass., 1939), cf. 64-5, 107-8.

E. Casady, "The Neo-Platonic Ladder in Spenser's 'Amoretti' ", *Renaissance Studies in Honour of Hardin Craig* (Stanford, Calif., 1941), 92-103, and *Philological Quarterly,* 20 (1941), 284-95.

R. W. Reese, "The Influence of the 'Song of Songs' on Elizabethan Literature", Diss. University of Washington, 1940, *University of Washington Abstracts of Theses,* 5 (1941), 93-5.

Ch. B. Beall, "A Tasso Imitation in Spenser", *Modern Language Quarterly,* 3 (1942), 559-60.

E. Bizzarri, "L'Influenza Italiana sugli 'Amoretti' di E. Spenser", *Romana,* 6 (1942), 626-37.

R. Gottfried, "The 'G. W. Senior' and 'G. W. I.' of Spenser's 'Amoretti'", *Modern Language Quarterly,* 3 (1942), 543-6.

A. C. Judson, " 'Amoretti', Sonnet I", *Modern Language Notes,* 58 (1943), 548-50.

W. V. O'Connor, "Tension and Structure of Poetry", *Sewanee Review,* 51 (1943), 555-73.

J. M. Bullitt, "The Use of Rhyme Link in the Sonnets of Sidney, Drayton, and Spenser", *Journal of English and Germanic Philology,* 49 (1950), 14-32.

S. Jayne, "Ficino and the Platonism of the English Renaissance", *Comparative Literature,* 4 (1952), 214-38.

M. Evans, "Metaphor and Symbol in the Sixteenth Century", *Essays in Criticism,* 3 (1953), 267-84.

169

D. Bludau, "Humanismus und Allegorie in Spensers Sonetten", *Anglia,* 74 (1956), 292-332.

V. Kostić, "Spenser's 'Amoretti' and Tasso's Lyrical Poetry", *Renaissance and Modern Studies,* 3 (1959), 51-77.

L. R. Sonn, "Spenser's Imagery", *ELH,* 26 (1959), 156-70.

N. Yuasa, "A Study of Metaphor in Spenser's 'Amoretti'", *Studies in English Literature,* 36 (Tokyo, 1959), 163-86.

R. Ellrodt, *Neoplatonism in the Poetry of Spenser* (Genève, 1960).

J. W. Jessee, "Spenser and the Emblem Books", Diss. University of Kentucky, 1955, *Dissertation Abstracts,* 20 (1960), 3729.

L. L. Martz, "The 'Amoretti': Most Goodly Temperature", *Form and Convention in the Poetry of Edmund Spenser: Selected Papers from the English Institute,* ed. W. Nelson (New York, 1961), 146-68, repr. *The Prince of Poets,* ed. J. R. Elliott, Jr. (New York, 1968), 120-38.

H. Smith, "The Use of Conventions in Spenser's Minor Poems", *Form and Convention in the Poetry of Edmund Spenser: Selected Papers from the English Institute,* ed. W. Nelson (New York, 1961), 122-45.

B. E. C. Davis, *Edmund Spenser* (New York, 1962).

W. Nelson, *The Poetry of Edmund Spenser* (New York, 1963).

L. Cummings, "Spenser's 'Amoretti' VIII: New Manuscript Versions", *Studies in English Literature, 1500-1900,* 4 (1964), 125-35.

R. Kellog, "Thought's Astonishment and the Dark Conceits of Spenser's 'Amoretti'", *Renaissance Papers* (1965), 3-13, repr. *The Prince of Poets,* ed. J. R. Elliott, Jr. (New York, 1968), 139-51.

W. F. McNeir, "An Apology for Spenser's 'Amoretti'", *Die Neueren Sprachen,* N. F. 14 (1965), 1-9.

Ch. G. Osgood, H. G. Lotspeich, eds., *The Minor Poems, Part Two,*= vol. VIII of *The Works of Edmund Spenser: A Variorum Edition,* ed. G. Greenlaw et al., fourth printing (Baltimore, 1966), cf. 417-54 and 628-44.

D. M. Ricks, "Convention and Structure in Edmund Spenser's 'Amoretti'", *Proceedings of the Utah Academy of Sciences, Arts, & Letters,* 44 (1967), 438-50.